Finding Rest for Our Souls
Stories of Soul Survivors

Amber Mattingly, Editor

with Amanda Clark-Hines, Andre Brown, Dawa Norbu,
Angela Patterson, Courtney Armento, Michael Esterheld

Energion Expand
Cantonment, Florida, USA
2024

Energion Expand
an imprint of Energion Publications
1241 Conference Rd
Cantonment, FL 32533
pubs@energion.com
https://energionexpand.com

Table of Contents

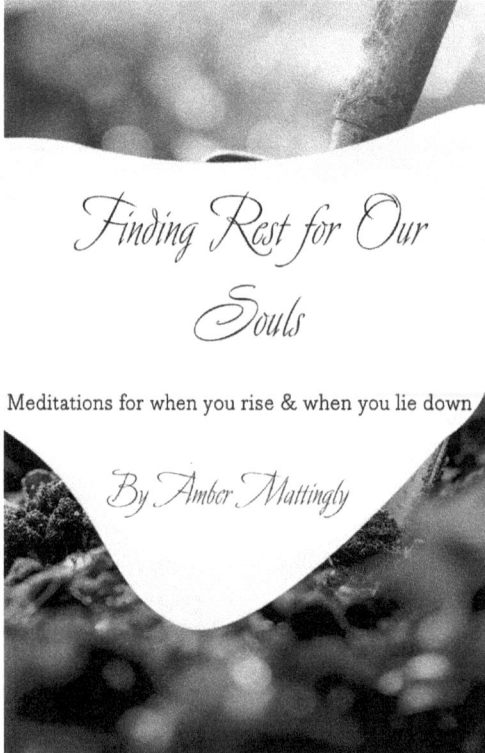

Finding Rest for Our Souls

Meditations for when you rise & when you lie down

By Amber Mattingly

This seven day morning and evening meditation on the Psalms is
available at: https://energion.com/7-day-practice.

Introduction

After completing my recent writing project, *A Leap of Interfaith: Finding Treasures Through Shared Practice*, with my colleague and friend Pema Lisa Antoniotti, I began contemplating how people establish a sense of safety within their religious or spiritual journey . This inquiry arose from discussions with Christians during our study on shared practices. Some Christians questioned why their tradition did not address building trust or finding solace, but rather assumed these aspects as given or at least implied.

Several personal crises in my life and a heightened awareness of the crisis of our planet, humanity, and religious institutions emphasized a need for stories of people who experienced hardships and yet found a sense of safety. During this time of personal and ongoing communal turmoil, I turned to the Psalms. Through this exploration, I discovered that the Psalms encourage us to embrace the full spectrum of human emotions. They prompt us to express our feelings openly, assuring us that God's love is vast enough to encompass all our thoughts and emotions. By engaging in this practice of sharing our deepest emotions with God and feeling fully accepted, we find solace and security within this relationship.

Once we have expressed our anger, fear, sadness, and desire for retribution, the Psalms redirect our focus inward. They encourage us to delve into our inner selves, a challenging journey unique to each individual. To aid in this exploration, I invited various authors to share their experiences and offer practices that guided them toward the peace they sought. These chapters and practices collectively birth what I term "the Inner Sanctuary." By introspectively examining our role in personal or communal crises, we strive to cultivate the same sense of safety, non-judgment, and peace that we find in our relationship with our Creator. Some may view this through the lens of seeking refuge. As understood by Christians, refuge provides a protective shield amidst life's storms, but conversations with people from other faith traditions have broadened my understanding of refuge. Refuge is also trusting in a source of direction, guidance, and assurance. Refuge embodies not only protection but also trust in a guiding light that steers us with wisdom and confidence. This holistic refuge encapsulates the respite we discover within the Inner Sanctuary. Crafting comfort within this sacred realm demands patience, attentiveness, and a steadfast intention.

What is truly remarkable about this book is that each author unearthed within themselves the very tools needed to flourish, and I believe you, our beloved reader, will too. It is my heartfelt wish for this book to serve as a companion on your journey, reassuring you of your kinship with fellow seekers. For thousands of years, people have quoted, chanted and sung the psalms to express the cry they feel emerging in the depths of their souls. As you read each story, you will find that the Psalms still speak to us today helping us navigate the path of suffering so that we might embrace new life!

My name is Amber Mattingly. I hold a Master of Divinity degree from George W Truett and in 2020 completed by Doctor of Ministry degree from Claremont School of Theology. My dissertation's title is "From the Pew to the Mat: Seeing and Hearing the Outsider." I focused on creating safer spaces for people from any or no religious background to engage in spiritual conversation. I am a yoga teacher with training in Ashtanga, Adaptive Yoga and Trauma informed yoga practices. I see the need for our religious traditions to be firmly rooted in practice as the gateway to expand our spiritual consciousness. I am a pastor of a Disciples of Christ church who through my leadership in 2022 decided to embrace new life through merging with a sister church instead of closing its doors. I am a mother to a neuro diverse child and another child who explores the world through music and theatre. I am the best friend & wife to the pastor of Kingwood Christian Church. My work with Middle school students and with those who identify as spiritually fluid was chosen by the National Benevolent Association (Disciples of Christ) to participate in the first Sent Cohort in 2021. In this work, I accepted invitations to be interviewed by Edge with the United Church of Christ and consult with In-Dependence a wellness community for military spouses. I value Beauty, Flexibility, Community & Collaboration. You can find me at ambermattinglylivefree.com.

Recently, I co-authored a book with my dear friend Pema Lisa Antoniotti titled A Leap of (Inter)Faith: Finding Treasures in Shared Practice. You can listen to the podcast about this project by locating Collaborate 2022: From Unknown Other to Sacred Other on Spotify.

Chapter 1

Amber Mattingly

The Path to Peace is Painful

I failed. When I say, "I failed," I mean that I failed beautifully, magically, and totally. And I was not young and it was not my first job. It all started when my children became old enough to attend school and I was itching to begin my career as a minister. During my children's early years, my husband and I realized that having a neurodiverse child required one of us to stay home until the advocacy for services outside of school and inside of school settled, so I chose to put my career on hold to focus on strengthening the support services. I volunteered as a children's minister at my husband's church and I filled the pulpit for area churches who did not have ministers, but my first paid position came years later.

I started as an Associate Pastor in a local congregation. On a stormy night, I interviewed and shared with the members in great detail my hopes and plans. They hired me and I quickly began working on my plans. We had a great 6 month honeymoon period and then things began shifting. Just like after a marriage honeymoon period when everything is magical and your partner can do no wrong and then all of a sudden you begin to get annoyed with how your partner squeezes the toothpaste or pretends to not see the film on the shower so that you do all the cleaning; this is how I felt treated by the church. I was wonderful one moment and then the worst human being the next moment. I did not understand what was happening so I mirrored the church's behavior and began to shift. I shifted my personality. I lacked confidence in putting actions to my plans. I dove deep into an obsession with people liking me. This only made things worse because I was being fake. The church did not seem to like me, but they really did not like the fake me either.

Two years after I was hired, I arrived at a Sunday night board meeting and resigned my position. It felt like a divorce. I agreed to continue working until a church counselor met with everyone to help us address our issues. In the end, staying was not an option for either side and I left my position. I cried for the next three years and my sweet husband held all of my grief. I had always wanted to go back to school for my Doctor of Ministry degree, so during this season, I entered Claremont School of Theology's DMin program that focuses on compassionate leadership. As I read material related to my Doctoral project, I found Ruby Sales' interview with Onbeing. Ruby Sales is a social activist and theologian who witnessed the shooting of one of her colleagues. He was shot because he was a white man standing in line behind a black woman. This was not the only defining moment in her life. In the interview, Sales talks about another defining moment. In a conversation with her friend's daughter, Sales felt guided to ask the question, "Where does it hurt?"[1] Sales told the interviewer that this one simple question set her friend's daughter free to share things that she had never felt she could share before. Later in the interview, Ruby Sales says that most people begin speaking about what they hate, but underneath this hate is a love that has been lost, taken away or stolen.

Ruby Sales question, "Where does it hurt?" sent me on a quest to explore my own hurt and my seemingly inability to stop crying about what happened in my first church experience. First, I needed to ground myself in the story of my call to ministry. Feeling that deeply rooted experience of being called to ministry strengthened my resolve during this painful time of reflection. I have a viv-

---

1   Ruby Sales, interviewed by Krista Tippett, "Where Does it Hurt?" On Being.org (September, 15, 2006) 7.

id memory of the moment I felt called. We belonged to a United Methodist Church when I was young and in this church, we had an elder named Peter who would joke about his name saying that he was the rock on which our church was built. Just a little church humor from Matthew 16:18! Peter was a large man in size and in personality. One day after worship, he asked if he could see my hand. I cautiously extended my hand, and he took his large finger and traced the palm of my hand. Then, he looked into my eyes and said, "You are a healer." At that moment, I felt very special, but completely confused by his meaning. Fast forward to reading the Ruby Sales interview and I think I was beginning to see the path in front of me. I needed to find healing so that I might offer sacred space for others to find their own healing. Healing sounds mystical and positive, but first you must suffer a wound. I learned as a pre-physical therapy undergraduate major, the second step in the healing process is that you must pick at the wound to clear away the debris. Well, I had suffered a great wound and now it was time to turn inward and ask, "Where does it hurt?" This is not a pretty process. Turning inward involves getting down and dirty in the bloody mess of the wound which makes it look worse.

One of my favorite authors and a man I consider a mentor for my ministry is Henri Nouwen. Nouwen describes the Hebrew word for compassion, *rachamim,* to mean "a movement of the womb of God."[2] The question rises, "How do leaders develop the compassion that moves a person at the gut level?" To begin this journey, Nouwen talks about this first step of turning inward. He sees this act of turning inward, these moments of solitude as "the furnace of transformation" where a leader confronts all the inner movements of the self.[3]

---

2   Henri J.M. Nouwen, Donald P. McNeill, and Doublas A. Morrison, *Compassion: A Reflection on the Christian Life* (New York: Random House, 1989), 14.

3   Henri J.M. Nouwen, *The Way of the Heart: Connecting with God through Prayer, Wisdom, and Silence* (New York: Ballantine Books, 2003), 15.

Nouwen wrote that as we face our personal suffering, we experience a feeling of connectedness with the suffering of all living beings. He and his mentor Thomas Merton[4] experienced suffering, turned inward in solitude to address the suffering, and afterwards felt an internal spaciousness to hold the suffering of others.[5] Nouwen was also very direct to Christian leaders, but I believe his statement is true for all people. He wrote that leaders must walk the path before inviting other people onto the path.[6] I interpret his statement to mean that our unique way to help others is to face our wounds, walk the spiral path to healing, and then return to help others find their own path to healing. There is a connection that happens between those who share their healing journey and those who suffer because they feel a renewed sense of hope that, one day, they will find their own path to healing. The one sharing the healing journey feels a sense of solidarity that inspires a deeper experience of compassion to bring relief to those who suffer.

But in my story, we are not there yet! Ruby Sales asked, "Where did it hurt?" Literally, I hurt all over my body. During my final year at my church, my autoimmune issues flared up and there were times that I could barely walk. My inner struggle was outwardly screaming through physical pain and I could not hide the effects. Continuing my journey inward, I worked with a therapist and the compassion-based curriculum at Claremont School of Theology aided in exploring new practices for healing. Internal work took me back to my family of origin to explore the systems that are in place that shaped who I am today. I can say that God created me to be bold, direct, and have the strength to follow what I know is right, but I also can say that my family of origin enhanced those innate capacities whether in rebellion of the system

---

4   Henri J.M. Nouwen, *Encounters with Merton: Spiritual Reflections* 2nd Ed. (New York: The Crossroad Publishing Company, 2004), 72-74.

5   Henri J.M. Nouwen, *Our Greatest Gift: A Meditation on Dying* (New York: Harper Collins, 1995), 32.

6   Henri J.M. Nouwen, *Wounded Healer: Ministry in Contemporary Society* (New York: Doubleday, 1972), 99.

or as a response to the system. This is not to say that I had a perfect home life or to blame my home life for the way I express myself in the world. I am acknowledging that family systems hold great power for better or worse.

On my path to healing, one of the easier avenues I explored was the shift I saw in myself while working at the church. I wondered why I was trying to be someone else which was not sustainable in the long run anyways. What I found was that I am more of a people pleaser than I had expected. Some people might say that I don't have a people pleasing bone in my body because I can be very direct in my language and strong in my direction of choice. Deep inside, I explored how I longed for a "mother-like" figure to be pleased with me and a "father-like" figure to see how hard I was working. I still see this show up today in surprising ways when I encounter certain personality types!

I grew up with a father who struggled with alcoholism and was a workaholic. Our home was not restful and we all struggled with sleep. My mom took care of the children and blamed my father for any problems that she experienced. I was her "defender and advocate," which made me her favorite until I entered college and realized that I wanted a better relationship with my father. Then, when a therapist guided me to share my desire with my mom and that I needed to put boundaries in place so that I did not hear everything negative about him; I was no longer her favorite. I was cast aside, and she chose her next favorite child. One minute I was special and the next minute, I was not. In many ways the experience at my church of being loved one moment and the villain the next moment offered me an opportunity to face this previous wound.

Taking the spiral to healing a little deeper, I became curious about my need to feel safe. For me, pleasing people was a symptom of just trying to feel safe in a changing environment. I recognized that in church board meetings that I did not feel safe to speak because when I did speak up, I usually had a different perspective and people would stare at me like I was an alien. This lack of safety affected my body. In my body, I noticed that I clenched my jaw the entire meeting and would leave the meeting with a headache. My experience at church was that it was not safe to be myself. It was also not safe to try and be someone else. I was not safe to be myself at my home of origin either. The story I was telling myself was that I was not pleasing; I was not safe.

Fortunately for me, my sisters introduced me to yoga 7 years earlier which was my first experience of truly feeling safe. I recognized that my suffering physically affected my body, while yoga relieved the suffering. Yoga fed my soul, brought clarity of mind, and gently released the tension I held in my body. I wanted to explore why this practice provided a safer place for me, so upon leaving my church position, I entered Yoga Teacher Training.

During my training, I began thinking about how creating a yoga community is like creating a church community. Like the church, yoga offers space for spiritual practices on many levels. People participate in church life for a wide range of reasons from engaging in church life because of family ties, for community support, and some hope that the church will help them connect to God. Similarly, there are many levels of connection to the practice of yoga. Some people practice yoga only for the physical benefits; some begin to realize the mental and emotional benefits; others hope for greater union with the Divine. Like churches, yoga communities offer service projects, book studies, and even potluck meals for fellowship.

I started considering the similarities behind preparing a Christian worship experience and the preparation behind creating a yoga class. Church and yoga include music, a ritual or plan to work through from beginning to end, community building elements, prayer or meditation, a message or theme, and a benediction or closing remarks. The idea occurred to me to begin preparing for and teaching yoga classes like I would for a worship experience.[7] Since leaving my formal ministry position and becoming certified

7   Amber Mattingly, *From the Pew to the Mat: Seeing and Hearing the Outsider*, (Doctoral Project. Claremont School of Theology, 2020) 7-8.

as a yoga instructor, I was surrounded by spiritual people who did not attend church. I wrestled with hoping to create a yoga class that is meaningful to their lives by physically engaging hurt stored in their body and offering them a loving message. Many people stayed after my classes to voice their appreciation of the message within the yoga class. One person voiced, "I don't go to church anymore, but your yoga class feeds my soul."[8]

This thoughtful journey finally got to the heart of the matter which for me was about safety. I began to be curious about why I felt safe on my yoga mat, but not as a leader at my church. I wondered why yoga students felt safe in my class, but not in the church. I realized that I was not alone in my feelings. There is a group of people with negative church experiences, but at the heart of the matter for many of us is that the church space was no longer safe. The practice of yoga taught me that there is an energetic quality to safer spaces; there is a smell, a sound, an invitation, and that the leader has an ability to hold the practice in a spirit of non-judgment.

The practice of yoga taught me about how my body responds to safer spaces. It helped me release the suffering from my body. As my body released the tension, my mind received the message from my body that I could become more flexible, more open, hold memories and ideas more reflectively. This practice on my mat helped create an inner sense of safety where I could treat my suffering with gentleness. I recognized that as I practiced yoga, my heart expanded to include all human beings who do not feel safe. Eventually, my heart had room for those individuals in the church who hurt me. Finally, I felt connected to all of God's creation as God's beloved. What Henri Nouwen said would happen, happened for me! My practice of yoga was a way through my suffering to opening space in my heart for the suffering of others. This did not happen overnight. Remember, I cried for 3 years. But I prac-

---

8   Amber Mattingly, "From the Pew to the Mat: Seeing and Hearing the Outsider," 9.

ticed yoga and meditation through my tears and let my mat hold
me with tender care.

Music helped me realize that my journey to healing involved
reflecting on my past and that it was shaping my present interest
in a ministry of healing. I listened to Lady Gaga's song "Million
Reasons" and heard the cry of my heart about the church in her
words. She sings about how she can find reasons to quit everywhere she looks, but all she really needs is just one reason to keep
going. I truly was begging God to give me just one reason to stay
at a traditional church setting. The traditional church setting did
not seem to embody the message that God created all human beings good, so how was I to make my way back to a place that I felt
a sense of rejection. Lady Gaga stepped in again and helped me
realize that my message is a simple one that must be shared repeatedly. "Born This Way" by Lady Gaga is a celebration of diversity
and an unapologetic toast to the courage that it takes to be yourself in this world. This would be my message and, as the comedian
Jim Gaffigan says, "It is so simple." It's so simple that we miss it.
It's so simple that we must hear the stories repeatedly. It's so simple
to those who have eyes to see, but a mystery to the blind of heart.

Another great album is from the movie The Greatest Show-
man! For me, this movie was the greatest sermon ever preached.
It touched all my senses and I stepped out of the movie theater
thinking that the movie captured a central theme in my denomi-
nation, yet we are not as excited or eager to share this message! My
heart still leaps when I hear Hugh Jackman sing to Zac Efron the
song, "The Other Side." In this song, Jackman asks Efron to leave
his money, family, and reputation to chart a new course. Efron is
not sure that there are any benefits to leaving his connections, but
Jackman sings that he will gain the freedom to dream and that he
will feel the effects in his body because his heart will expand and
his mind will be open to new possibilities. Every time I hear this
song, I just want to jump up and say, "Yes!" For too long, people
have defined God's love too narrowly, but as the heart space expands, there is an infinite pool of love for all living beings. When

I started teaching, I practiced teaching yoga with the message of this movie: that all of God's creation bears the image of God and is good. I practiced looking into the eyes of my students and seeing God in them. So, when an opportunity presented itself, I was ready to expand my heart even more.

I participated in a project at Claremont School of Theology where I learned a practice from an individual of a different faith tradition. During my time at Claremont, I had befriended Pema Lisa Antoniotti, a Tibetan Buddhist Monk. I asked her to teach me a practice and I asked that the practice be deeply meaningful to her if she was given permission to do so. Pema taught me a meditation that I practiced daily and journaled my responses. In my first solo practice, I wrote in my journal about feeling a deep level of fear that was healing. Pema and I met to talk about my response to the practice and she asked about the fear. The fear that I experienced was deep and we both thought I must have carried this fear for years. The rest of that first journal entry said that I "laid down after the practice and felt light, lifted, floating. I felt safe, truly safe...like a homecoming."[9]

> Pema wrote about my experience in our book, A Leap of (Inter)Faith. Pema wrote, "Amber later shared that the most significant benefit of the practice came regarding intimacy, perhaps on both the spiritual and intrapersonal levels, "As the practice has gone on, I am imagining that I find myself opening and allowing, and it is a wonderful freeing feeling." What struck me the most was the intimacy she described *within* herself, as if she felt such a deep sense of safety that she could reconnect to her *whole self* and also to something greater. In response, I recalled the ways traumatic events can be disconnecting and shaming, and Amber's statements led me to ponder how the *relational safety* might help some practitioners heal from the more severe effects of trauma.

---

9   Amber Mattingly and Pema Lisa Antoniotti, "A Leap of (Inter)Faith: Finding Treasures in Shared Practice" Topical Line Drive, Vol 46 (2022), 22.

I continued meeting with my therapist during this six-week project and at the end of one of our sessions, I arrived at the source of my struggle to feel safe with myself, in God's beautiful world, and with God. This awakening took me back to my time in the womb. I do not remember this time myself, but during a conversation with my mom, she opened my eyes to an intention she created for my life before I was even born. I was conceived so that my mother would feel safe in her home environment. She thought that if she was carrying a child that she would be safer at home. So, the intention for my life was that I was to be a protector, a defender, an advocate for those who cannot advocate for themselves. On the one hand this is a beautiful intention to live into. On the other hand, I was a child who grew up without a sense of safety for myself. My family was not safe so the larger world did not feel safe. If I was to protect and defend, who would care for me? If I no longer wanted that role, would I still belong to the family unit? I asked myself how much of who I am did God create me to be and how much of who I am was wrapped up in the intention my mother set for me. Through a brief study in Internal Family Systems Therapy, I began to picture myself as an infant, tenderly holding this image of myself, and giving her the freedom to choose her own path. The practice of yoga and the meditation Pema taught me were instrumental on my path to healing, so when Pema invited me to be a co-researcher on a more expansive study of this Buddhist meditation practice, I knew that Jesus as my teacher and healer would rejoice at my choice to offer a way to set others free.

Pema and I decided to expand our research to include a larger population. We gathered a group of Buddhists and Christians and taught them the practice. The Buddhists learned the traditional version and I taught a version that Christians could adapt to fit their faith tradition. The group practiced for six weeks with daily journaling and regular group meetings. During this project, some of the Christian participants commented about feeling a new sense of safety. Here is what we found.

Within the relational effects of the practice, two themes emerged that were quite different from the Christian participants' previous experiences of practices found within the Christian tradition. First, the idea of feeling safe with God, Jesus & the Spirit emerged as a new experience. One participant wrote, "I felt gratitude for the safety. Don't recollect Christianity focusing on feeling safe." Yet another participant noted, "I enjoy the focus on the Trinity. I felt the I-Thou relationship with the Godhead, noting a sense of joy and awe that I could be in relationship with the Ground of All Being. I'm still feeling a sense of awe and immense gratitude. (He asked) "Who are we that God is mindful of us?" He stated, "I felt safe in God's presence, nurtured, cared for, loved, appreciated. Like the love of a mother, unconditional."[10]

The study was intense and as we read the journals, I noticed many experiences with the Christian participants that mirrored my own experience. It was an exciting time to think about the possibilities of shared practice between different faith traditions and how we might be able to heal and grow spiritually together! Then, our entire sense of safety in God's beautiful world was threatened by covid. I write covid in all lower-case letters because we have given it too much power in our lives. The pandemic threatened our physical bodies, our mental abilities, our emotions, and our ability to sustain meaningful connections with each other. According to HAI Global, the study of neurobiology and social psychology informs us that humans are wired to connect. The latest neuroscience out of UCLA tells us that the drive for connection is as essential to our wellbeing as our basic needs of food, water and shelter. The study reminded me that in 2016 the US Surgeon General said that citizens of the United States feel lonely. The warning was that this is an epidemic of loneliness. Four years later, the world faced a global pandemic that forced us to physically distance ourselves to protect each other from this deadly virus.[11]

10   Amber Mattingly and Pema Lisa Antoniotti, *A Leap of (Inter)Faith: Finding Treasures in Shared Practice*, 36.

11   Susan Rutherford and Kate Gillespie Ed. "Connection is Essential to

I am not here to judge how anyone handled the pandemic. On every side, I saw people suffering and making decisions that helped them relieve the suffering even if just for a moment. On every side, I saw fear driven by people not feeling safe in their bodies, in God's beautiful world, and questioning their ability to feel safe with God. For me, I spent most of the pandemic creating art with my children, walking the 77 miles of trails in our community, and teaching yoga online. I thought I was fine, but I had not tested that sense of safety quite yet. It wasn't until I needed to see my chiropractor that I was truly tested. When I entered my chiropractor's office, I noticed that no one was wearing a mask. This was only two months after the world shut down and I was not expecting this response although my state officials said we no longer had to wear masks unless the business requested that we do so.

So, there I sat in the chiropractor's office with my mask on in a near panic trying to quiet my breath and slow my heart rate. As I sat waiting to be called back, I remembered a short meditation which I had recently read about in Thich Nhat Hanh's book "Together We are One". In this book, he wrote about the first months of his exile and how he felt like he did not have a home. He was on a tour traveling through many cities telling the truth about what was going on in Vietnam and in each new city he would wake up disoriented. He writes, "When we have the feeling that we are not accepted, that we belong nowhere and have no identity, this is when we have a chance to break through to find our true home."[12] What he realized during the first years of his exile was that he was teaching the principles of his tradition, but that these principles had not yet sunk in. The truth that he would come to realize is that finding your true home has nothing to do with feeling at home, accepted, or a sense of belonging in any one place, but finding your true home has everything to do with fully living in the present moment. For me, I talk about it like this…finding my

Survival." HAI Global (www.hai.org/connection-is-essential-to-survival)
12   Thich Nhat Hanh, *Together We are One: Honoring our Diversity, Celebrating our Connection* (Berkeley: Parallax Press, 2010), 12-13.

true home is creating an inner sanctuary where I can rest in God's presence feeling truly loved and accepted for who God created me to be. It's an inner space that is open, kind, and accepting of whatever I am experiencing at the moment.

On that day in the chiropractor's office, I decided to try one of the meditations that Thich Nhat Hanh offered in his book. It reminded me of a mantra that I chose on my own to repeat at night. At night I say, "I am safe. I am loved." This meditation from Thich Nhat Hanh was to help me connect to that inner sanctuary that can be accessed wherever I go and it invites me to stay in the present moment by repeating the words, "I am home. I have arrived." I sat in the chiropractor's waiting repeating the words, "I am home. I have arrived. I am home. I have arrived." And before I knew it my body softened and I was no longer fearful, but instead felt the joy of the present moment. This is what safety feels like for me: detachment from being emotionally hijacked, peaceful mind, softened body, free spirit. This embodied experience is how I know healing has taken place. Now, this knowledge shapes the message and ministry: there are paths, peace is possible, and healing is purposely painful.

Practice

I began my journey with the practice of yoga. This is not where everyone begins, but this seems to be a good place to start especially because human beings live an embodied experience. The body is an amazing tool for discovery and transformation. The body experiences our thoughts, emotions and actions, and holds the memories of those experiences. Sometimes we forget that we are a human living in a body and think that the body is somehow disconnected from our life experiences. When our brain sends messages to the body, then the body sends messages back to the brain. In my experience, I wanted to feel safe in God's beautiful world with God's good people, but first I had to feel safe in the smallest land that I occupy, my body. Then to expand my ability to feel safe no matter where I was located, I created a more expansive feeling in the tight spaces of my body so that the body would send a message to the brain that I am safe. This also affected my heart space and I noticed that my compassion grew to include a larger circle than just myself. Now, no matter where I find myself, I can connect to my breath, soften my body, my mind and heart softens, so that I find rest.

If you are willing to give it a try, here is a link to my You-Tube Channel. Enjoy the free classes! https://energion.co/amber (https://youtu.be/lTaYVT-gS6A).

Chapter 2

From the Pew to the Mat and Back

After 4 years working in the yoga community, I found myself open to working in a traditional church setting again. When I wrote my clergy profile so that our churches could read about me and consider me for an interview, I wrote about our open stance. As a Disciples of Christ minister, I am called to live into creating a safer space that is founded on One Creed. Our one creed is that we believe that Jesus is the Christ, son of the living God, Lord and savior of the world. In my profile I wrote, "This posture reflects the gospel's idea of "being saved." This is the idea that salvation is not a one-time act of confession, but an on-going process of learning and living, un-learning and living, re-learning and living. In this way of following Jesus, humility becomes a key attribute of faithful people."

I interviewed and accepted the position as solo pastor of a local congregation. I had new tools in my toolbelt from my Doctoral program, yoga teacher training, and the meditation practice. I felt safe in my own body. With all these tools and the time I spent creating an internal sanctuary, I thought I could handle the regular stressors of ministry. We began our time together studying Henri Nouwen's Life of the Beloved so that I could share with them my passion for ministry and how I view my role as their pastor. I was who God created me to be. I was still direct in my speech and strong in my choice of direction. Yet, I learned to listen not just to my member's words, but at a deeper level for the heart of the matter. I used my yoga teacher training to attune myself to the messages of member's body language and to invite them to listen to themselves. They grew to love me, and I grew to love them. We had a great honeymoon period that lasted five months.

After five months of settling into the role, tragedy struck and she struck hard. It all began with a training that I attended through our regional office. I entered the training completely un-aware that I would learn that my beautiful church was in financial trouble. I took lots of notes and could have kept what I learned to myself. I could have prioritized our relationships and the history of our church in the community. I could have kept my mouth shut to keep my job. But that is not who I am, so at our next board meeting, I presented my findings and asked that they take a few months to explore the reality of our situation. I prayed that my limited understanding of church finances through this one training was incorrect. I know they prayed similarly.

I was not wrong. The news devastated all of us. Surprisingly, I felt safe even though things had shifted more quickly than in my first church experience. I felt at peace even though I knew we had a painful process to go through in the next several months. I wondered though how I would help this community through their suffering. I was new enough to the community that I did not have emotional ties to our property or to our traditional form of ministry, but I knew this would take thoughtful planning to help my members face their pain. So, I leaned heavily on Henri Nouwen's advice that leaders must walk the path first before they invite others. I trusted that I was walking my own path to healing and that I had learned some things along the way that might be help-ful. Through my doctoral project, I received feedback on creating safer spaces so I returned to that project's findings to guide me in this new opportunity. Also, I recognized that my own suffering opened space in my heart to hold the suffering of my people in compassionate care. I knew that I was sent to my people and that as painful as this process would be, this challenge would continue the spiral of healing.

My next step was to offer a ten-week discernment process to work through our emotions, understand our options in detail, and prayerfully discern where God was calling us to go for the next season of our ministry. This part of the process is like picking the debris from the wound that I mentioned in the last chapter. It is painful, a bloody mess, but necessary for healing. The key for the discernment process to work was to create a safer space so that people felt seen and heard. I returned to a summary statement from my doctoral project for guidance. Through the feedback process of my project's participants, I saw a theme emerge that gave insight into how to create safer spaces especially when there is significant difference present. In my Doctoral project, I wrote, "When words feel <u>expansive</u> and <u>inclusive</u>, I feel the <u>freedom</u> to be me and <u>share </u>my <u>experience</u> while <u>listening </u>helps me understand my <u>uniqueness</u> in the group and <u>connectedness</u> to the group that inspires <u>hope</u> for the future."[13] One of the tools that helped my participants in my doctoral project feel safe enough to participate was reading the intentions of how we are going to relate to ourselves and each other before every gathering.

I referred to my doctoral project's theme crafting expansive and inclusive discernment practices and questions. I created opportunities for small group and larger group listening sessions. I challenged my members to share their thoughts and ideas within a guideline of attention to time so that those who are quieter would be given an opportunity to share. Before every meeting in the discernment process, we read a list of seven promises that we made to each other as we discussed this sensitive topic. I used this tool to create a safer space, but also as a reminder for all of us to look into each other's eyes and see God. This process was challenging because I could see and feel the tension in some people. I heard their sadness, anger, and disbelief in the process. Through it all, I

---

13   Amber Mattingly, "From the Pew to the Mat: Seeing and Hearing the Outsider," 112.

did not take it personally. They were grieving and I was just the messenger. I felt connected to some of the stories of the prophets in the Hebrew bible who had to deliver terrible messages that no one wanted to hear. Yes, I was not alone in this calling and at least God did not call me to cook my food over my poop as a sign of shitty times ahead! Just a little bible humor from Ezekiel 4:12.

My own suffering connected me more deeply to my people. We were a faith community with people at various stages of grief and some experiencing compounded grief since we were still in the pandemic. All of us were on a spiral of healing which included many untold stories that this new experience touched in a deeper way. I did not try to be someone else or feel the need to please. My practices heightened my awareness of my need to feel like I am doing a good job. I began to be aware of the moments when I was trying to prove my worth. Another awareness that I was continuing on the spiral of healing.

After ten weeks of meeting together every week for discernment, we took a two week break to be quiet and pray. Then, we took a vote. We had three choices to choose between: Plant a new church, Merge with a sister church, or Create a plan for Sustainability so that we can stay on the property. The first two options would force a sale of our property where we had been located since 1926. The third option allowed for some creativity within the not for profit status of the church. I was proud of my members for diligently participating in the process. I was grateful for their effort and the responsibility they showed. We worked hard together. We listened well. We cared for each other during the week so that we held the group together with love and encouragement. Although we did the work, the vote was tied, so we did not make progress in deciding our next steps forward. What we did do was eliminate one of the options. We were not going to plant a new church. No matter how much I would have loved to plant a new church, the decision was unanimous, and it was the right decision for the personality, temperament, and energy of our members.

After our vote, the discernment process took a pause. I called every household to speak with them personally about what they would like to see happen next. Eventually, these phone calls crafted our discernment process, Season 2. After a six week pause, we began to meet again, but this time not everyone participated. I started making phone calls and the truth was that many of our people did not want to continue this painful process. Their energy waned. So I decided to look at the previous vote to see how those with energy voted. It was clear to me that all of the energy voted in one direction so I informed the leadership of this reality. The group decided to take another vote. This time the vote was for merging with our sister church. The following week, we met with a grief counselor to better understand how grief touches other experiences in our lives and how to recognize behaviors that we use to help us cope with our grief.

Feeling unsafe in this world has something to do with loss, loneliness, and sometimes a sense of displacement. It does not have to be extreme like Kya's experience in Delia Owens' novel *Where the Crawdads Sing*. Kya experiences family members leaving her one by one over a long period of time until she is finally alone. At the young age of 6, she learns how to cook, clean, and care for herself. Kya chooses to stay away from the community because her community kept her at arm's length because she was different from them. For Kya, human beings were not safe, so she stayed away to maintain connection to her land and way of life. Her story is one of many ways we feel unsafe in this world. My church felt unsafe because their land would be sold and they would suffer feelings of displacement. One by one, we were being forced to leave the land that saw over 100 years of ministry in our community. Even though we had examples of communities of faith in our situation, we felt alone navigating our way forward. We felt like a people without a home. We were selling our property and moving to a new location, but we had not fully arrived at the new location. It felt like we were leaping into the air knowing where we wanted to land, but we had not touched ground on the other side.

What I did not know was that an even greater personal tragedy sat like a heavy cloud ready to burst over my family. As I
searched the Psalms to help my church navigate the emotions
currently present and those unskillfully hidden in passive aggres-
sive actions, my husband experienced burnout in ministry as he
pushed through his last few months before his first sabbatical began. So in the middle of lent, we took a family trip. We all needed
a break. On this break, Chad and I spent one night away from our
children to celebrate our 21st anniversary while our children were
cared for by people we knew and trusted.

Our little break ended, and we headed back to our home state
to set a date for my congregation to begin worshiping as a new
church family with our sister church and to finish the final months
before my husband's sabbatical. We were excited because it looked
like I was going to be able to join my husband for more of his
sabbatical since the timing was lining up for my church to begin
the merger process during the month of Chad's sabbatical. Our
sister church already had an intentional interim minister in place
to help guide the process, so my responsibilities would transition
to mainly administrative duties. My hope was to use the sabbatical time to prayerfully discern if I felt called to apply for the new
pastor position of the merged church family or if I felt my time of
mutual ministry with this congregation was complete.

Three days after arriving home from our short break, our son
who is neurodivergent shared with his friends that he experienced
inappropriate touch while on our family break. I was sitting at
home reading for my upcoming sermon when I answered a phone
call. A mother of one of my son's friends who I did not know called
me to let me know what information my son was sharing with his
friends. I could not breathe. It was 9am and I would have to wait
until 3pm to talk with my son. I spent the entire day thinking
about how this could have happened. I sat staring at a blank wall
with my mind frozen in fear. We were protective parents who took
our time to check out everyone in our children's lives. We were the
parents who went with our children to our church's sexual educa-

tion classes and participated in open discussions with our children at home. We were the parents who made sure our neurodivergent son knew what inappropriate touch meant.

The minutes ticked by slowly but finally my son walked through the door at 3pm. I greeted him, made him a snack, and invited him to talk with me about something very important. He looked up at me and said, "I know what we need to talk about." Over the next 3 months, our son shared more with us and with his counselor. This had not been a one-time incident but the abuse spanned over the past two years. From the moment our son shared with us about his experience, we listened and let him know how courageous he was to speak the truth. We gave him space and time to process out loud with his counselor and with us. We all experienced a shift of energy as the magnitude of this truth soaked into our beings.

I felt like my world had turned upside down. My first Sunday in the pulpit after my son's announcement, I arrived at church without having slept in five days. I pulled my leaders aside and cried through the brief telling of my story. I did not know if I could lead in worship. I could not imagine giving my sermon that morning. I was shaking from head to toe. My sweet leaders hugged me and said, "If you can't do it. That is ok. Just give us a look and we will have an all-sing Sunday!" We began church and I was doing just fine until the special music. Our musicians had chosen the song "Come What May" by We Are Messengers. I cried as I heard the words, "Sometimes sorrow is the door to peace. Sometimes heartache is the gift I need. You're faithful, faithful in all things." Really?! On this Sunday, I would have to trust the writer of those lyrics and allow the message to unfold over time. After the special music, I stood up, walked to the pulpit, and delivered my sermon on the Psalm. What I could not imagine was possible gave me the gift of using the energy of my grief for comfort and healing my congregation. What I thought impossible opened an opportunity for me to rely on a strength beyond my own abilities. My sermon may not have inspired anyone else, but it offered healing to me.

In a group I am involved in that focuses on Curiosity, one of the participants asked about how you know that you are done healing from a particular situation. As I sat there reflecting on the question, I realized that my experience offered some insight into her question. During my time at the first church, my therapist and I were exploring family systems. I was exhausted remembering all the work that I previously did with a therapist during college and I felt discouraged in that I was right back where I started all those many years ago. I shared my feelings with my therapist, and she responded with great wisdom. She said that the path of healing is more like a spiral. We heal and then something happens, and we wind back around not to that same place but maybe we are given an opportunity to revisit an experience at a deeper level. I recognized my own tendency to set a goal: healing. I needed an amount of time: 6 months. Now, I can check it off the list and move on, but what my goal and time limit did was create more suffering when a new experience resurfaced my old suffering. If I could see healing as a spiral, then I could recognize that each time an old wound popped up, I was being given the opportunity to view it from a different perspective. I learned that if I can view healing as a spiral then I am less discouraged with the thought that I did not do the healing process right the first time. Instead, I would feel open hearted to another opportunity for healing.

The way we treat ourselves and each other has consequences. Sometimes we visibly see when someone is hurting themselves, but often the signs are missed because the wounds are internal. Same is true for when we hurt each other or hurt Mother Earth. Sometimes we experience loud and measurable consequences, but often the silence cuts through our hearts at a deeper level. The Psalms express this type of enduring truth. I did not realize that the Psalm I preached on the Sunday after my world turned upside down would speak to me. I wrote the sermon weeks in advance and only had the final editing to complete. My Psalm on that Sunday was Psalms 62: 1-11

My soul waits in silence for God alone; From Them comes my salvation. God alone is my rock and my salvation, my stronghold; I will not be greatly shaken. How long will you attack a man, that you may murder him, all of you? Like a leaning wall, like a tottering fence? They have planned only to thrust him down from his high position; They delight in falsehood; They bless with their mouth, but inwardly they curse. My soul, wait in silence for God alone, for my hope is from Them. They alone are my rock and my salvation, my refuge; I will not be shaken. My salvation and my glory rest on God; The rock of my strength, my refuge is in God. Trust in Them at all times, you people; Pour your heart before Them; God is a refuge for us. People of low standing are only breath, and people of rank are a lie; in the balances they go up. Together they are lighter than breath. Do not trust in oppression, and do not vainly rely on robbery; If wealth increases, do not set your heart on it. God has spoken once; Twice I have heard this: that power belongs to God; And faithfulness is Yours, Lord, for You reward a person according to their work.

As I preached my sermon, I realized this passage held three messages for me. First, I had spent a considerable amount of time in silence staring at the wall. I had no thoughts. I moved very little. My breath was shallow. This is not my normal behavior. I speak up. I take action to help relieve the suffering. I am flowing with life and breath. Now, the first 2 days, I was still operating like myself, but then there was nothing left to do yet everything felt uncertain. So, there I sat. The Psalms spoke to me by reminding me that my sitting in silence was not an act of surrender or of giving up. No! I was waiting for my soul to tune into God's presence. I was waiting for my nervous system to recalibrate. God would provide the strength I needed when the time called for more action. I can sit in silence and stare at the wall because this was an act of hope!

As I waited in silence, I felt my frozen brain re engage. With my brain back on board, I recognized it was time to explore some inward movements. I turned to Henri Nouwen's words again,

"In solitude we realize that nothing human is alien to us, that the roots of all conflict, war, injustice, cruelty, hatred, jealousy, and envy are deeply anchored in our own heart. In solitude our heart of stone can be turned into a heart of flesh, a rebellious heart into a contrite heart, and a closed heart into a heart that can open itself to all suffering people in a gesture of solidarity."[14]

This might be shocking, but I took his words seriously and began to investigate my own heart for times that I have been unkind to my son. The guiding thought I gleaned from Nouwen's writing was that if I could find the root of the injustice done to my son in my heart, then my heart would soften and I could offer compassion to the one who hurt my son. Well, I found plenty of examples throughout my years of caring for my son. I found resentment towards my son for having to give up my career to care for him when he was young even though I had a choice. I remembered times when my resentment bubbled up in words that were unkind. I wanted him to be grateful for my sacrifice; he was oblivious. I wanted him to see that we always put his needs above our own; he was never satisfied and wanted more. I protected him as best as I possibly could; he struggled to understand why this experience happened to him. This was not an exercise in self-hatred, but a way to come down from a position of feeling like I am better than human beings who cause harm to others. I found enough of the roots of cruelty within myself that I could soften my heart toward my son's abuser knowing that God created us in God's image and God called us good. I see a lot of goodness in myself especially because anytime I spoke harshly or treated my son poorly, I recognized my error and asked for forgiveness. I know I modeled this pattern well because my son mirrors this pattern in his relationships.

---

14   Henri J.M. Nouwen, *The Way of the Heart: Connecting with God through Prayer, Wisdom, and Silence* (New York: Ballantine Books, 2003), 25.

Let's be fully human right now. The second thing I appreciat-ed about this Psalm is that the writer spoke about his enemies. The writer calls them attackers and writes that they delight in deceit. The Psalmist says that people who hurt the vulnerable are lighter than breath. Now, I had much uglier words for the person who hurt my son, but I also loved them. I wanted people to believe my son and to acknowledge this challenging person's deceit. I wanted justice for my son and felt compassion for the suffering experi-enced on all sides.

The Psalms teach us to pour out our hearts to God in the best times, worst times, and everything in the middle. Open the Psalms and the raw humanity of the writer's words leap off the page. There are passages where the writer is asking God to kill his enemies and then the Psalmist is begging for forgiveness. The Psalmist offers beautiful descriptions of God's tender care and gut-wrenching expressions of feeling God's absence. Truly, the full range of human emotions are present in the Psalms which provides comfort knowing that God holds it all together. When I explored the Psalms, I began to feel that I was not alone and that my faith community who was grieving was not alone. Our ancestors of the faith suffered exile from their land and did not have access to their temple. Some of the Psalms write about feelings of disconnection and dislocation from God which is a feeling my community felt strongly. The music of the Psalms reached out and grabbed my heart just as the songs of our time connected to my experience of a broken relationship with the church.

The Psalms are the sacred songs of the ancestors of our faith tradition, but my view of what is sacred includes seeing God's creativity in the gift of what some people call secular music. As I processed my feelings about my son's experience, my Spotify ac-count picked up on the emergence of my darker side. I noticed a Moody Mix appeared on my home screen. Some of the songs on this list touched me deeply, opening the floodgate of healing tears. One day I pressed play on the Moody mix while I was working on my art in the garage at my work bench. The song "Exile" by Taylor Swift came on and suddenly I felt the truth of her words. My family was experiencing what it is like to be exiled from those we thought loved us because we told the truth. My son's voice was not heard or believed because he is neurodivergent. The signs of abuse were dismissed, and his voiced truth treated as disloyalty. Sadly, I had seen this film before.

Other songs offered a sense of solidarity with those who suffer. That spring our daughter chose to sing Billie Eilish's song, "No Time To Die," for a concert at the High School and at the time I thought it was really dark, but as I played the song out in the garage I recognized a similar emotional tone in myself. Ed Sheeran's song, "All of the Stars," described perfectly the distance created by living miles apart from and what it feels like when there is emotional distance, but the hope that the stars "will guide us home." For my family, the exile we experienced was in the miles between us, but it was the distance in our hearts that felt the most challenging. It was Kelly Clarkson's song "Piece by Piece" that gave me the courage to face the truth of my son's experience, connect it to my life story and the story of my extended family. Her ability to craft a beautifully heart opening, empowering song about her life experience invited me to use my voice in the writing of this book. Songs have the power to connect us to our own experience and to others in solidarity. Songs have the power to change us by opening our heart to the life experience of people who are not like us. Songs have the power to challenge us to feel our pain and use that energy for good in the world. I was beginning to recognize that our Psalms hold this same power.

Lastly, Psalm 62 reminded me how hard it is to trust. I thought about trust and how the ability to trust as an adult depends on the formation of secure bonds in childhood. I looked over my life and clearly saw the signs of an avoidant insecure attachment style. This attachment style has difficulty forming close relationships. Yes, that is me. People with an avoidant insecure attachment style seem independent. Yes, that is me too. I remember as a young child when my father would come home from one of his many business trips that instead of running and giving him a hug, I would look over my shoulder, give him a look that said I did not care, and then turn my attention back to what I was doing. I also fit the last part of the avoidant insecure attachment style because I have always had a hard time recognizing my emotions. When asked how I feel, my answer is, "I don't know." My process is to receive incoming information, choose an action based on my gut feeling, process it thoughtfully, and maybe someday arrive at the emotional level.

For me, trust blossoms over time and through multiple experiences. Even though my avoidant insecure attachment style with human beings made trust difficult, my many life experiences and the readings of my sacred text affirm that God is trustworthy. The Psalmist gives us insight into why God is trustworthy. He writes that God has power and that God is faithful. This reminds me of a word that I have loved since seminary: *hesed*. I even named my first business, Hesed Consulting. *Hesed* is used 250x's in the Hebrew Bible and ½ of those times, you find it in the Psalms. Sometimes in the Hebrew bible, *hesed* is translated as faithfulness, but it is a faithfulness out of generosity and not out of obligation. *Hesed* is also translated as loyalty, but it is a loyalty which embodies mercy. The root of the word *hesed* means to bow one's head towards another in a covenantal relationship. You can think about it like this…in covenantal relationships there are rights and responsibilities for both parties. But in the case of a covenantal relationship between humans and God, God is *hesed*. God's character is a generous faithfulness and God's loyalty is full of mercy. So, we as the other party in the covenantal relationship can find a sense of safety and rest in the relationship because God does not just offer or promise *hesed* and then can take it back at will. NO, God is *hesed*. No matter what happens God's faithfulness is generous towards us. No matter where we find ourselves God remains mercifully loyal.

Now mix *hesed* with God's power and you have a God worthy of your trust. What this means to me is that as Creator God calls

God's creation good, the natural progression would be for God's power to sustain that goodness by working to bring about good in this world. And not only is God's power oriented towards creating good even out of the complexity of human experience, but God's desire is to see all things work together for good. And so we can join the Psalmist in saying, "God alone has the power and desires to work all things for good. So my soul waits in silence for God alone;"

The idea of God as a refuge is written repeatedly in the Psalms, but I don't think the Christian community has taken these words seriously enough. We say "trust God" but we have very little understanding of how life's experiences shape a human being's ability to trust. We say God is trustworthy, but we don't want to hear all the stories of human suffering that threaten that very idea. When some Christians see and hear the myriad of stories of great suffering, they end up walking away from the faith tradition which informs me that our teaching is not deep enough to reach into those dark places. Therefore, it is time to turn to the Psalms. It is time to be fearless in shining a light on the full range of human emotions so that we might strengthen our ability to feel safe with God, each other, and in God's beautiful world. Let's get down and dirty with the Psalms so that we might find the rest that we need for our souls.

Practice

Let's begin to turn inward and create an inner sanctuary. What does that mean and how might one do that? Great questions! First, do you want to sit or go for a walk? Great choice! Now, set an amount of time on your phone so that it will chime when your practice is complete. Whether sitting or walking, begin to tune into the sights around you. Try to just notice without giving running commentary in your mind. You are practicing tuning into the world around you without judgment of good/bad, beautiful/ugly, too bright/dark. Next, try softening your gaze by releasing any tension in the muscles around your eyes. You can even gaze down or close your eyes if you are sitting. Please don't walk around with your eyes closed! Now, tune into the sounds that you hear without judgment or getting lost in a story about the sounds.

Let's turn inward. Tune into how your body feels right now. Remember to shift from judging to observing the sensations of the body. Are you cold/hot? How does the sun feel? Where do you feel the flow of air on your skin? Do you feel tension somewhere? What places feel soft and open? You might find yourself drifting into commentary like, "I feel tension in my shoulders. I think it is because I slept on my side which I know I should not do. Maybe I did not sleep very well. I remember a dream..." If you find yourself wandering down a thought path, that is ok! It is what the mind was created to do. The awesome news is that when you recognize you have drifted, then you have returned to the practice. You have observed your mind wandering!

Coming deeper into the inner sanctuary, observe the emotions that are present today. Observe your tone. Notice your energy level. Now, use the words from the Psalm to fill this inner sanctuary with peace. Repeat the words, "God is my refuge" or any other word that gives you a sense of safety. Repeat this phrase at a comfortable pace. Maybe it matches the pace of your breath or your footsteps. Repeat this phrase until you feel the truth of the phrase fill your body. When you are finished, take a moment to rest in that fullness.

Chapter 3

The Dirty Mess of the Psalms

I was sitting in a Christian conference when I heard the speaker talk about how humanity is being called to take another big step forward in spiritual consciousnesses towards harmony. This speaker talked about how we are in a moment in history where our ability to take the next step into harmony is about our survival. He separated out the many crises that we are witnessing today. As I sat there, I silently added to his list that we are facing a personal and communal crisis of dislocation and disorientation when it comes to who to trust for our information and how to talk about the complexities of our experience. This speaker is not the only person talking about this huge change that we are going through. Some writers are saying that we are the midwives of a new way of being. Others are saying that there is a rise in Christ Consciousness that might be a new way of interpreting the second coming of Jesus.

As I listened to the idea that we are being called to the next level of spiritual consciousness, I remembered that I had read similar words about a different period in history. In the book *Chanting the Psalms*, Cynthia Bourgeault writes, "Fascinatingly, the period during which the bulk of the Psalms are thought to have been composed (800-200 B.C.E.)—corresponds exactly with a time in world history known as the axial period. Universally and apparently spontaneously, human spiritual consciousness seemed to take a dramatic lunge forward."[15] As I read her words again, I re-

---

15   Cynthia Bourgeault, *Chanting the Psalms* (Bouler: New Seeds, 2006), 11.

alized that if the Psalms had a role to play in the axial period, then they might offer us insight for this next step forward.

In looking at the axial period, Bourgeault offers us insights that just might touch a similar place that we are at today. During the axial period the major world religions began shifting from communal responsibility to individual accountability. The Psalms span the entire period of this great shift, so it is easy to see examples of tribal membership language and the emergence of the language of a people who are experiencing individual freedom of choice. The latter represents this large shift. The Psalms brought us a new language, the language of the emotions, as our people processed this shift in thought. This shift opened a new way of relating with God. The writers poured their hearts out to God in real and raw words that reflected a more complete view of the human experience. The writers did not shy away from stating exactly how they felt! Then, our people began to sing and chant and pray these words. This was new territory that the ancestors of our faith were charting and that today we might take for granted.

I felt comforted knowing that we have been in the middle of a giant leap forward before and found our way through new patterns of thinking and reconstructing deeply beloved practices for new use. Our shift is different in many ways though. In the Axial period, we were shifting away from tribal membership to individual freedom and accountability. This is an important shift, but this next giant leap in spiritual consciousness is equally important. Harmony calls us to recognize that our freedom of choice affects our neighbors and our planet. We are not isolated individuals, but we can trace how we are interconnected to all living beings. Harmony guides us to see the world as God's creation and to care for this world as we care for ourselves. Harmony asks us to see our neighbor's happiness as essential for our own wellbeing. Harmony begs us to start with turning inward and looking at ourselves including taking seriously what we fill our minds, hearts and bodies with so that we not only walk the path of peace, but embody peace.

As I look around, I don't see signs of harmony emerging, but if I can step back and see that we are in the middle of a leap forward, then what I see is resistance. Someone once said to me that resistance can be grief in disguise. If I can be curious about looking at our resistance as grief, then maybe what people are grieving is the change that they feel but may not be able to articulate. Change is hard and it feels comfortable to stay with what we know even if what we know is hurting ourselves and all living beings. I would say that the heart of the matter is that people are resisting and grieving the change because they do not feel safe. Many people do not have a theology that says that God created our world and called everything good like our Sacred Text says in Genesis 1. In this same chapter, God created humans and called humanity very good. Instead of seeing our world through the lens of innate goodness, many of our people only see the world and other humans as innately sinful. This does not create a feeling of safety. Instead, it creates a feeling of fear of other humans and fear of God. When we don't feel safe, we just want someone to tell us the rules for how to keep God on our side so that we feel protected. We hide and disconnect from our safety concerns by quickly solving our feelings of discomfort through following the rules.

The Psalms for Today

The question I have been pondering is "What can the Psalms teach us as we face this next shift?" Let's dip our toe into some of the themes found in the Psalms that might comfort us today. This is not an exhaustive study on the Psalms. This is not a commentary. This is real life, real world, my life and your life meet the Psalms today. So, I am going to share with you what I have encountered in the Psalms that speak to my life and invite you to continue the process by exploring these and other themes found in the rest of the book for yourself.

First, let's explore the path of the Psalms as a whole. The Psalms help me feel a sense of solidarity with our faith community. We have been in a shift before, felt uncomfortable, grieved the loss, and wrote these words to express our sense of dislocation and disorientation. Not only do we feel a communal sense of solidarity with our people because they experienced a shift before, but there is a deeper, more personal level of solidarity that we find with the psalms. The Psalms are like opening the personal prayer journal of a people. If I am feeling something and wondering if anyone has ever felt this way before, then I can open the Psalms and realize that I am not alone. When the Psalms are read, prayed, chanted, or sung, the words invite us to explore their meaning for our own lives. When we engage the Psalms in this way, there might be a feeling of connection to the words of a particular psalm which is a way of praying the words as our own. There is also a sense of reaching out to be held by the larger faith community who through the years have sensed a connection to these words. We are talking about words that live in the collective consciousness of our people and when we attune our spirit to the words, we feel their power across time and space.

Cynthia Bourgeault points out that Jesus quoted the Psalms in his greatest moments of suffering not only to express his own suffering, but to "give larger context to his own experience."[16] We see evidence of Jesus reciting the words of the Psalms in the 3 gospels Mathew, Mark and Luke where Jesus recites Psalm 22:1, "My God, my God, why have you abandoned me?" or in the Gospel of John where Jesus says, "Father, into your hands I commend my spirit," from Psalm 31:5. Jesus had the words of the Psalms printed on his heart so that in his moments of deepest suffering these were the words that bubbled up as a way to express his own emotions in the moment while transcending the moment to remain connected to the communal experience of his people.

Second, the Psalms give me permission to feel the complexity of the human experience. The writers of the Psalms expressed both positive emotions and emotions that we might say should not be expressed publicly. The writing of the Psalms shows us this

---

16   Cynthia Bourgeault, *Chanting the Psalms*, 16.

new thing that God is doing in the life of the people of our faith tradition. The writers found a new way to express the emotions of their complex human experience. They wrote in a form of poetry that could easily be sung with words that shock us, words that we recognize have bubbled up in our own hearts, and words that helped them release pent up emotions. As the writers expressed their complex emotions, they learned that the far away God who cares for all God's people is also intimately close to the thoughts and feelings of individuals. The thought becomes, "God loves our whole community and God calls me God's Beloved!" For me, it seems like two sides of the same coin. When we follow the Psalms and get down and dirty in expressing our complex emotions, there is a feeling of God's acceptance which leads to a sense of safety.

Cynthia Bourgeault says, "What I believe happens when we introduce the psalms into our consciousness—and even more so into our unconscious—through the practice of contemplative psalmody is that they begin to create a safe spiritual container for recognizing and processing those dark shadows within ourselves, those places we'd prefer not to think about."[17] I like to think about this spiritual container as an inner sanctuary. I began to feel the creation of an inner sanctuary when I stepped onto my yoga mat. Not only did the mat provide me a physical space for my body to move and breathe, but as my mind focused on my breath pattern, I began to sense an inward movement. This movement was a shift away from paying attention to everything and everyone around me, to paying attention to what was going on inside of me. As my teacher guided me to practice not judging where my thoughts went or how my body felt or what emotion was present, I was creating a kinder and more welcoming environment. Then, when things popped up that were ugly or painful or sad, I had a safer space to process my shadow side. This is also the path that the Psalms invites us to explore. It is a path that leads to the creation of a safer inner sanctuary. We need this space so that we can feel safer no matter where we find ourselves. Then once we feel this inner

17   Cynthia Bourgeault, *Chanting the Psalms*, 43.

sense of safety, we begin to look out at the world through a softer, kinder, and more gentle lens.

The inner sanctuary is a space of non-judgement, non-harming, and non-attachment. As this space is created, we find rest because our inner dialogue is more kind. We also notice a change where we no longer need to resist anything or push anything. We can let things rise to our awareness and notice when something new replaces the thought from a moment ago. For me, this changed my relationship with suffering. I recognized that suffering is a part of life, but that it does not have to take up all the space in my life. When I am experiencing suffering, I can also experience great joy and the reverse is also true in that when I am overjoyed, suffering might also be present. When I began to feel this sense of safety in the inner sanctuary is when I noticed an excitement rise within me about turning to help others find their own way to create an inner sanctuary. The overflow of the goodness inside of me eagerly desired to create a world where all beings feel safer.

The psalms give us a way to connect to ourselves, to connect to the larger community of our faith tradition, and to connect to God in a more intimate way. As we connect to ourselves, we create this inner sanctuary where we are safe to explore the wide range of the complex human experience. Creating an inner sanctuary brings God closer because we find that God has always been and will always be present in the inner sanctuary. The writers of the Psalms begin to use words about experiencing a more intimate relationship with God. God is the shepherd, the one who washes us clean, the one who created us, the one who knows everything about us, the one upon whom we call to come in defense of us. So, let's begin with this theme of safety and see how the Psalms address how we find a sense of safety with God.

God is our Refuge

In many of the Psalms, the writers share that God is our refuge. Now, I did not hear many sermons or participate in many

conversations about how God is our refuge in my churches growing up, but I know we sang a few songs that held this message. I
am sensitive to words in songs and confess that I won't sing songs
in church anymore that talk about God's love is like a hurricane
because I live in Houston where the last hurricane devastated our
area! A hurricane is not a safe place for me. I'm not sure what I
thought the phrase God is our refuge meant, but I can definitely
tell you what it is not. I might have thought that there was a shelter somewhere out there where God would keep me safe. I know
that I thought the church should be a safe place. Taking refuge
had something to do with a place out there different from where I
found my body on most days. But what if all along God resides in
me as I am their image bearer and as I grow into more of their likeness? What if as I grow into more of their likeness, I experience a
greater sense of who "I am that I am" is to me? I see the writers of
the Psalms guiding us through a process of discovering who God
is for each of us personally and how God invites us to act as their
image bearer in the world. Let's not take for granted the Psalmist
idea, but let's dig into what case the psalms build for the premise
that God is our refuge.

First, the Psalms tell us that God is our refuge because God
is *hesed*. I have already talked about the word *hesed*, but I want
to give a beautiful example of how the word *hesed* impacts our
wellbeing. In Psalm 42, the psalmist writes, "Why are you cast
down O my soul, and why are you disquieted within me? I will
put my hope in God; for I shall again praise God." This Psalm was
written during the time of exile when the people had lost their
land, their temple, and their sense of community. Orienting the
Psalm during the time of exile, we can hear both the despair of
God's apparent absence, but the memory of God's previous acts
in history bringing the psalmist back from the pit of despair and
into desiring God again…even hopeful that he will praise God in
community once again.

There is tension in this verse, and we know it well because
it is a part of the human experience. The tension human beings

hold is the emotions of living in a time of feeling God's absence in the horizontal world while recognizing that the horizontal world is not our full reality. As God's people, we also live in the vertical space of the Kingdom of God that gives us solid ground on which to hope that this feeling of God's absence is momentary, fleeting, impermanent.

While this Psalmist soul is downcast, he is also experiencing the taunts of his enemy. He writes that his enemy asks him, "Where is his God?" One commentator wondered if the writer's enemy might be himself. If we become curious about this idea, then we might say that the writer is turning inward to question a part of himself. He is being brutally honest about his own "internal grappling with faith to an external wrestling with faithlessness."[18] I think this brings the Psalm to a new level of appreciation because it is a part of human nature to have this internal battle going on when life has not gone as planned or we are not living according to the values we hold most dear.

The Psalmist shifts from despair to hope in verse 8. "By day the Lord commands steadfast love, and at night God's song is with me, a prayer to the God of my life." I love the idea that God's song is with me at night. Gives me images of going to sleep reciting or chanting the psalms or that I might wake in the night with the words of the psalms on my lips. This is an example of how God's *hesed* impacts our wellbeing. No matter what happens, God's faithfulness is generous towards us. No matter where we find ourselves, God remains mercifully loyal. So, when the part of us who doubts cries out, "Where is your God?" The other part of us can respond, "By day the Lord is faithfully present and at night God's song is with me."

I have a friend who recognized that the worries and stress of daily life were leaving her with a sense of overwhelm. She confided in me that she was so consumed with horizontal living that

18   Richard Blake, "Psalms 42 and 43" in *Feasting on the Word: Preaching The Revised Common Lectionary*, Year C Vol 3, eds. David L. Bartlett and Barbara Brown Taylor (Louisville: Westminster John Knox Press, 2010), 157.

during the day, she lost connection with the reality that we live in a vertical space as well. So, she created a practice. She set her phone to chime several times throughout her day. She decided that every time the phone chimed that she would pause, breathe, and remember that God is with her. This practice of "waking up" to a more expansive view of reality throughout the day soothed her anxiety and gave her a new perspective on life. Her story reminds me that God is *hesed* and that if I want to experience God's faithfulness and loyalty then I must engage the reality of God's presence in our world. My friend may always need her phone to chime at her or with practice she might "wake up" on her own throughout the day. A safe place to find rest is available, but we must wake up!

Another lesson I receive from the psalms is that God is our refuge because God is the Creator. By this, I don't mean a one-time Garden of Eden Creator. What I mean is that God's creative power is at work in our world. In Psalm 62, we hear the writer is suffering from the attacks of his enemies. He writes that his soul waits for God. Then, in verses 5-10, he tells the community to learn from his story. He wants his experience to inspire them to trust in God's creative power at work in the world. Follow the line of thinking: Creator God calls God's creation good and God desires this good work to continue in the world, so God's power sustains God's creation, so that we might bring about good in this world. And not only is God's power oriented towards creating good even when humans make a mess, but God's desire is to see all things work together for good. And so we can join the Psalmist in saying, "God alone has the power and desires to work all things for good. So my soul waits in silence for God alone;"

The psalmist in chapter 62 wants the people to hear his story so that they can learn from his experience. Remembering the stories of God's work in the world is a practice that helps us trust in God's *hesed* and creative power. Psalm 78 and psalm 107 invite us to cast our gaze back to the many ways God's goodness was expressed in the world in the history of the people in our faith tradition. Psalm 78 mentions how God's people forgot God and disobeyed, yet God was faithful. Psalm 107 praises God for God's goodness and outlines the many times throughout history that God saved the people. The Psalms hold the collective memory inviting the readers across time and space to remember and then to add our own stories which helps us look back at God's creative power at work in the world today. This practice gives us hope that God's goodness will express itself in creative ways in the future.

God's *hesed* and creative power at work in the world wake us up to the reality of God's presence with God's creation. In Psalm 139, the writer says that God, "searches and knows" every part of him. God knows his daily habits of sitting and standing. God knows the words that have yet to come out of his mouth because God knows his heart. The Psalmist proclaims in verse 6, "Such knowledge is too wonderful for me; it is so high that I cannot attain it."

In the first six verses of Psalm 139, the psalmist says that God knows all of his daily activities. Then in verses 7-12, the Psalmist delights in knowing that God's presence is always there. There is nowhere that we find ourselves where God is not already there to welcome us. Henri Knight said it so beautifully. He wrote, "Such a text beckons like an old friend. On the long passage through the wilderness, it stands like a familiar and oft-visited way station, a place of refuge and renewal on the difficult way."[19] A major emphasis here is that God is ever present and that it takes our turning our attention to God's presence. It's like a dancer who is dancing to the music unaware that their movements are being held, supported, and strengthened by a dance partner. The magic happens when in a difficult pose, the dancer turns their face towards this previously unseen presence. It's a moment that takes your breath away!

---

19   Henry F. Knight, "Psalm 139:1-6, 13-18" in *Feasting on the Word: Preaching The Revised Common Lectionary*, Year C Vol 4, eds. David L. Bartlett and Barbara Brown Taylor (Louisville: Westminster John Knox Press, 2010), 35.

God's presence is always with us because God is *hesed*. *Hesed* is the idea that God is generously faithful and mercifully loyal to God's creation. So, God will not abandon us if we, as the Psalmist says, "take the wings of the morning and settle at the farthest limits of the sea" because God is generously faithful. If we find ourselves in the best of situations or sitting in the pit of hell, God is there because God is mercifully loyal to us. God's presence with us is connected to God's *hesed* and God's *hesed* moves God to work for good in the world.

Reading Psalm 139: 13-18, the writer is saying that God's presence is connected to *hesed* and it is intimately linked to God's power. God's power created light out of darkness. God's power created all things, and they are all good. And through God's sustaining power we experience God's love, care and concern. The writer is doing something very profound in this section because most often the writings of the time keep God high in the sky as Lord, King, Ruler, Provider. These titles keep God as a Creator that creates and then steps back from Creation. But in this section of Psalm 139, the writer explores the idea that God not only shows care and concern for all God's creation, but God is intimately involved in the creation of one human being. D. Cameron Murchison wrote about how this Psalm expresses the power of God's love through speaking of a Creator who is like an artist carefully shaping a single human being, one piece of art, in the depths of the earth."[20]

Through God's presence with us, God intimately knows us, but Henri F. Knight suggested that God's knowing is enhanced through the attention we give to God. He imagined that God acts as a divine host welcoming all parts of life, all parts of us, even those parts of us that refuse love's way of operating in the world.[21] So God as a host does not force or coerce or stalk us, but

20   D. Cameron Murchison, "Psalm 139:1-6, 13-18" in *Feasting on the Word: Preaching The Revised Common Lectionary*, Year B Vol 3, eds. David L. Bartlett and Barbara Brown Taylor (Louisville: Westminster John Knox Press, 2009), 84.

21   Henry F. Knight, "Psalm 139:1-6, 13-18" in *Feasting on the Word:*

God stands ready for our arrival with dinner made and a mint on our pillow allowing us to freely come and go as we choose. Just like how I lay my yoga mat out and keep it out to remind me to practice. There are days that I walk by and feel the invitation, but I keep walking because I am too busy or just don't feel like it. The yoga mat laying out in the middle of the floor does me no good unless I step on the mat. Once I am on the mat, then I need to do a little more than just go to sleep. The practice of yoga is simply to move and breathe, but I do have to move and breathe. Then if I fall asleep in the practice, I receive the sleep as a gift! Like the yoga mat, God's presence is with us and God delights when we turn our attention to the relationship.

The writer of Psalm 139 steps back to marvel at all that he has written about God's knowledge, God's presence, and God's power. We hear the writer feeling a deep sense of amazement, awe, wonder, and adoration in verses 6, 17 and 18, "Such knowledge is too wonderful for me; it is so high that I cannot attain it..How weighty to me are your thoughts, O God! How vast is the sum of them. I try to count them—they are more than the sand; I come to the end—I am still with you."

I am putting pieces together from various psalms that teach us things about ourselves and about God so that we can experience a sense of safety where we can find rest for our souls. We experience God's *hesed* as generously faithful and mercifully loyal. We see God's creative power at work sustaining the goodness that is already present in the world. We know God's presence is with us. All these aspects of God are wrapped in wrapping paper with a big white bow on top that proclaims God's abundant love. Guess what? We have a psalm for that too! Every year, the lectionary invites us to study Psalm 36 on Palm Sunday and I think it is because it is about how human beings experience God's Big Love. In reading the first four verses, one might think that this text isn't

---

Preaching The Revised Common Lectionary, Year C Vol 4, eds. David L. Bartlett and Barbara Brown Taylor (Louisville: Westminster John Knox Press, 2010), 37.

about love at all and that is because the writer begins the Psalm with an unloading of all the messy stuff of life. The Psalmist is human and having a momentary tantrum. What is coming up is not pretty, but he feels safe enough to bring even this shadow side of himself to the inner sanctuary.

I remember when my son was 7 and we were shopping in Walmart. He was not having a good day and we got into an argument about buying or not buying something and he threw himself on the floor in the middle of the aisle. I tried to calm him down, but nothing worked so I quietly said to him that I was going to continue my shopping on this aisle and that when he was ready, he could join me. This is how I picture the Psalmist! He is having a tantrum in the middle of the aisle at Walmart and God's love is Big Enough to hold space for this moment too!

A few months ago, I was throwing myself a pity party about having to always be the truth bearer and that no one likes the truth bearer. Boo Hoo. I even told someone that I am done with God's assignment and that I am going to close my eyes so that I don't see anything and I am going to close my ears so that I don't hear anything because telling the truth leaves me outside of the family of faith and it leaves me outside of my extended family. That is the story I can get stuck in and deceive myself into believing. When I get stuck, I perceive that this scenario is repeatedly happening even when it is not. But what another part of me was whispering was, "The truth shall set you free, Amber. The truth shall set others free, Amber. Come with me, Amber, & the truth shall set all free." I think God knows that sometimes we need to unload or upload, instead of reloading or ruminating on all the frustrations.

Once the junk is unloaded in Psalm 36, then the psalmist quickly turns to God's Big Love. In verses 5-9, we read that God's love and faithfulness are so enormous that they extend beyond the clouds and beyond the heavens. And so we begin to expand our small idea of God's love that includes my tribe or my faith community. We recognize that ALL is not just one big block of people but even includes specific love for me, little bitty me. And we discover with great joy that ALL includes ALL meaning that the ones who deceive others with their words that the Psalmist just wrote about in the first 4 verses. Yes, they are included too. All means those who don't live where I live or vote how I vote or believe how I believe or love how I love or think how I think or look how I look. All people can find a safe place to rest in God. We see God's power that is working for the good of All Humans and the Psalmist includes All Animals. We read about God's knowledge of our need for food, shelter, and water and that God is attentive to our needs, giving us an abundance of food, an ever flowing river from which we can drink, and that God's house is big enough to hold ALL people. This reminds me of the text in the Gospel of Luke where Jesus expands All even further. He said, "Even the rocks!"

The Psalm ends with the Psalmist asking for God's continual *hesed* and God's continued power to protect him from being led off the ancient path. We can see quite clearly that the writer of this Psalm was all over the map in his emotions. He went from a tantrum to having this epiphany of God's Big Love and then immediately doubts that God's love will continue in the future. And if you read and study the Psalms as a whole, you will see that the Psalms remind us to look backward and remember God's *hesed* as seen in the Exodus experience. The Psalms invite us to look back at Genesis 1 and hear of God's power to create. The Psalms invite us to look back and remember Genesis 12 where God speaks to Abraham about God's desire to know us.

Remembering is a great practice, but sometimes it isn't enough. When I am getting down and dirty struggling through hard times, I lose sight of what it means to trust in God. So I pray prayers asking for *hesed*, power and protection to be there in the future. This is not wrong. It is just who we are as human beings. Trusting is risky. And so, we need experiences today that remind us of God's Big Love. God's love must be made real in our human experiences. That is why I love the children's book Guess how much I love you because when you read it to your children you are communicating God's Big Love to them in a way that can be humanly experienced. Another way of communicating God's Big Love through human experience is in our intimate relationships. Katy Perry's song "Unconditionally" was written about a romantic relationship where she was trying to communicate her unconditional love for this human being. Her words touch my heart so deeply that I know that God's Big Love was expressed through her as she wrote this song.

Try to read the words of the song like a modern-day psalm about God's Big Love. The words of the song talk about how intimate relationships expose the messiness inside of us, but that a Big Love sees through the mess to the beauty buried deep inside. Katy Perry begs her beloved to step towards her in the fullness of human glory so that her beloved might turn his face towards her recognizing her presence supporting him in good times and in challenging times. These words speak of *hesed*, creative power, presence, and love. Can you hear this song in a new way?

The Psalms offer us a way to find rest for our souls, but the process is not just through intellectual assent. I don't think we can just understand why or how we should feel safe. I think we must participate in the practices that create safer spaces. The Psalms explored in this book show us that the path begins with giving voice to the complexity of emotions that we store inside. We need a way to release these emotions so that we can fully acknowledge all that we are carrying. Cynthia Bourgeault writes, "You begin to see and trust that what emerges from your unconscious during those times of "unloading" and shadow work is not overwhelming or isolating because others have walked this way before, and prayer upholds you as it did them."[22] Cynthia found her practice in Contemplative Psalmody and I found my practice in yoga.

No matter what the practice looks like, a part of creating a safe container for whatever shows up inside is purification. Purification is about releasing all the stored emotional junk and the psalm that best expresses the cleaning out process is Psalm 51.

22   Cynthia Bourgeault, *Chanting the Psalms*, 45.

The context of Psalm 51 is when David's affair with Bathsheba was discovered, and their love child is about to die. Remember that David took another man's wife, tried to hide his action by sending her husband to his death on the battlefield, and now thinks God is punishing him through the death of their child. The words of this psalm are very intimate. David asks God to, "Wash me thoroughly from my iniquity, and cleanse me from my sin...Purge me with hyssop, and I shall be clean; wash me, and I shall be whiter than snow..let the bones that you have crushed rejoice!" Michael Lodahl suggests that we imagine David lying naked before God like the writer of Hebrews 4:13 suggests.[23] Hebrews 4:13 reads, "And before him no creature is hidden, but all are naked and laid bare to the eyes of the one to whom we must render an account." The image is one of vulnerability before our Creator and reminds us of God's ability to bring into the light the things we try to hide.

The cleansing process unloads all that we store inside so that we can see more clearly. A part of this unloading is stepping back and seeing the things we are so wrapped up in that become like white noise. Once we see the junk that comes up, we remember that we are not alone. Others have felt this same way, done similar things, and needed a time of inner cleaning. This sense of solidarity with others shifts us off our high horse where we see others' junk as worse than our own. Instead, we stand eye to eye with our loved ones, strangers, and even our enemies. Suddenly, we embody a new sense of humility. Through this practice, our compassion grows. Then over time, we begin to mirror the qualities of our Creator: our faithfulness becomes more generous towards others; we embody a loyalty that is full of mercy; we use our creative power for good in the world; our presence is full of peace; Our love expands to include all... even the rocks! This is the path that will help us make the next giant leap forward in spiritual

23   Michael Lodahl, "Psalm 51:1-17" in *Feasting on the Word: Preaching The Revised Common Lectionary*, Year A Vol 2, eds. David L. Bartlett and Barbara Brown Taylor (Louisville: Westminster John Knox Press, 2010), 10.

consciousness. This is how we arrive at harmony within ourselves and in our world.

My son recently introduced me to a song that creatively explores the interconnection of experiences in our lives and the journey to simply seeing the way in which we are all connected. Interestingly enough, it is a country song called "A Rock" by Hardy. The song begins talking about how when we are young the world's complexities swirl around us, but we are unfazed because we simply want to see how far we can skip a rock. Then, as we grow life's challenges put us between a rock and a hard place. The song progresses as the character matures to thinking about loving someone else and starting a family. The character sees himself starting down this path by buying her a rock. The song brings the character to the end of his life when your burial plot is capped with your name being written on a rock. Finally, the song returns to the simplicity of the rock. Here is where the writer ushers in a bit of harmony. The artist sings that "We're all just living life on a rock." In this one song, the artist takes us from the simplicity of childhood through life's complexities and ends with a way for us to see that we are all in this together. Brilliant!

The brilliance of the song is that it makes the journey sound so simple which in some ways when the journey leads to discovering the heart of the matter, most of the time it is simple. But each of our journeys to the heart of the matter is anything but simple. There isn't a magic pill that works for all people. I am not endorsing some newly discovered practice that will take your mind to another dimension. I am talking about rediscovering an ancient path where you can find rest for your soul. Many people have walked this path. It is well-trodden, but what makes it interesting is that it is not just one path that leads us there. There are many paths but few who have searched to find their own unique path. In the next chapters, I want you to hear stories of people living today who have found their path.

The invitation is always there. The yoga mat is laid out in the middle of the living room. We stand ready to welcome you with a good meal and a mint on your pillow, but you have the freedom to come and go as you like.

Will you join us?

Practice

I attended a gathering with the United Church of Canada in a virtual meeting on the topic of Grief and Curiosity. During this conversation, Robert Dalgleish the executive director of Edge spoke about how the Psalms and Lamentations are resources for lament and resources for when we are dealing with change. Later, he offered a cleansing ritual. I have adapted the ritual below.

You will need a bowl of water, a sponge, and a second bowl that is empty.

Take the sponge in your hands and think about the sponge as your heart, mind, and spirit. Repeat the phrase until it fills your entire being, "Have mercy on me according to your great compassion."

Now, plunge the sponge into the bowl filled with water. Allow the sponge time to fill up to max capacity.

As you watch the sponge fill, think about all the things that burden your heart, mind and spirit. Feel the heaviness of the sponge as the heaviness of your being. Are you at max capacity or is there still space inside of you that is free of burdens? Feel the water that fills the sponge and notice the water that escapes because the sponge is already too full. What is "escaping" your life because you are too full or not in tune with a longing you have?

Repeat the phrase, "Have mercy on me according to your great compassion" until you feel complete.

Now, move in front of the empty bowl. Wring out the sponge so that all the water empties into the bowl. As your hands squeeze the sponge, imagine your body, mind and spirit being set free from your burdens. As you feel the water leave the sponge, feel that you are letting go of those burdens. When you are ready repeat or sing the phrase, "Create in me a clean heart and renew a right spirit within me."

Repeat this phrase or any phrase until you feel a release in your being.

Amanda Hines is a graduate of George W. Truett Theological Seminary where she earned her M.Div. and earned her certification as a spiritual director.

I'll be writing about my own journey with mental/emotional health and how it affected my relationship with Christianity and the Church. I hope to tie-in encountering my mental/emotional health through time spent in spiritual direction while looking at Psalm 13 & 42.

Chapter 4

Amanda Clark-Hines

Wholly Listening, Holy Listening

*I*magine this: you move to an entirely new place where you have no close connections to friends or family, it is the first time you are really on your own, the expectations placed on you are incredibly high, and you are still expected to grow and flourish personally when everything around you feels like it could change instantly. This is what life looked like as I moved several states away to begin my master's degree at seminary. I lived with a person I had a loose connection to, but I do not think either of us would have referred to each other as friends yet. I left a place where I had an amazing community of friends, a church that I could call home, and a season of my life where everything felt like it was in its place. Things back then felt certain and secure, and all of the transition and newness I faced made me feel like I could barely keep my head above the waters.

Many people affectionately call events like the one mentioned, "a season of transition" and one thing you should know about me is that I do not thrive under transition. Transition has always been a word that makes me uncomfortable because inevitably, it means that things are changing, whether it is an internal or external change. There is also no telling how long this transition period will last. It could be a few weeks, months, or even years to finally find my footing in a new environment and place. In the past, transitions brought me to seasons of deep hurt and pain. However, I recognize that transitions have the ability to offer seasons of powerful growth. My story of transition, feeling lost, and finding my way back to God offers pain and heartache but also transformation and restoration.

As I prepared to move to Texas for graduate school, the summer leading up to the big move felt like nothing but transitions. Transitions in location, friendships, and ministry and professional settings. Not to mention, right before I moved, I got dumped, and I mean floor-ripped-out-from-underneath-my-feet kind of dumped. It all served as a perfect recipe for internal turmoil, doubt, and uncertainty. I kept trying to assure myself that God called me to continue my education at a theological institution in order to prepare me to be a better minister. Unfortunately, my inner dialogue had never been one to comfort me during times of transition and uncertainty.

Maybe you are the type of person who speaks kindly to yourself. Maybe you are able to give yourself motivational speeches in your own head to hype you up before something big. Maybe you are a laid-back person who is able to go with the flow and shift easily when changes occur. I am here to say that I am not one of those types of people. The words I speak to myself are often critical, teetering on harsh. I tend to focus on the things that need improvement more than the things that went well. And when changes in plans occur, I find myself floundering and ruminating on my own inability to adapt easily. I often tell others that I am my own worst bully. And to be honest, I don't always like who I become. So, what does a deep fear of transition paired with the inevitability of change leave me with? I think it offers a space of pain and heartache where I wonder where God is in the messiness of life, and also it offers a space to reconnect with my own humanity to see that God grants healing, redemption, and restoration.

For most of my life, I would say that I operated with a relatively positive outlook on life. I was not naïve to the pain and suffering this world offered, but I also felt firm enough in my understanding of God, Christ, and the Holy Spirit to know that there is something hopeful on the other side. There's always a silver lining, right? For a small moment, this silver lining positioned itself in the excitement of trying something new, but even that wore off when the shiny newness eventually dulled into a dark reality.

Nowadays, I am more comfortable talking about my mental and emotional health, but I used to never address those things in my life, especially if I was trying to make a good first impression. It seems that many people still struggle articulating their own mental health and emotional responses. Perhaps it is still taboo to open up about things like that. Or maybe it comes from the false narrative that we cannot show our emotions, especially the "bad" emotions because it makes us seem like irrational people that are not put together. I have witnessed people apologize for crying in front of me or others. I would typically try to evade my emotions by busying myself, so then on the outside it just looked like I was being productive. I could not afford to let trifle things like emotions get in the way of chasing after what I deemed as successful or worthy of my time and attention. I treated success, contribution, and productivity as my own forms of currency and anything that hindered those three things were pushed aside to deal with at a later time.

Imagine your closest friend or your spouse speaking awful things to you about yourself. I'm talking about really insulting and demeaning things that would cause others to feel insecure and dehumanized. If a person you trusted told you that you were worthless, that the work you do will never amount to anything meaningful, or that something about yourself is inherently broken and unfixable, hopefully a different person in your life hearing those things would have the wisdom to advise you to end the relationship. No one needs that level of toxicity or negativity in their lives. Now, what if this person that speaks unkind things to you is actually you? As I got older, it became harder for me to find the silver lining when it came to my own self-criticism. I think at a certain point, I allowed my own criticism and harshness to just find a comfortable place in my life because I figured other people did the same thing as me. I never really addressed my words with myself, let alone tell other people and risk them thinking that something is wrong with me. I kept my feelings to myself, and no one would have access to them, not even me.

My first semester of seminary was honestly pretty good. Academically, I knew I would do fine because I was willing to work hard and put in the necessary effort. Socially, I struggled to make friends as I was not sure who was really a genuine, authentic friend. Like any formal education setting, I entered with a large cohort of people that I would see multiple times throughout the week as many of us took the same classes. My own roommate at the time was in three of my five classes. It seemed like some people became my friends out of a mere proximity principle rather than an actual getting-to-know-who-they-are-as-people kind of friends. I assumed this is how most people felt, and we all silently agreed that this would be the norm. I had some days where I doubted my qualifications, my credentials, and my reasons for being at seminary, but at this point, I had learned which sides of me I would allow people to see, and which sides would stay hidden. The side of me that had doubts or feelings of unworthiness would be kept hidden, and the side of me that contributed to thoughtful discussions and excelled in the classroom was allowed to be on display. When those feelings of inadequacy would creep in, I would mentally try to work through what was bothering me, maybe have a good existential cry before I went to sleep, and then wake up the next morning as if nothing happened. On the outside, I did well in my courses, I found a church that appeared to have all the right things, I got involved in a small group to "feed my soul," and I had a small group of "friends" I would hang out with weekly to fulfill any social quota I subjected myself to.

As my second semester of seminary progressed, I found myself at odds with my own mental health more frequently than ever. I never thought how the experiences of my own mental and emotional health could connect with my spirituality. Up to this point, I had trained myself to be a master at compartmentalizing areas of my life where my struggles with mental and emotional health were not allowed to touch my spiritual life.

Theological anthropology is concerned with the doctrine of what it means to be human. In the Bible, the basis of what it means to be human finds its place in the person of Jesus Christ to articulate and communicate that being a human depends on the concept of psychosomatic unity – that humans are creatures that are always both physical and spiritual. When it came to my mental and emotional health, I unknowingly took a page from the philosophical playbooks that advocated for a hierarchical dualism where my spiritual life was kept separate from my physical life. I had convinced myself that the physical sides of my life – the depression, the anxiety, the spiraling inner dialogue – were the messy, unbecoming parts of myself that needed to be separated from my spiritual life that was supposed to be fruitful and faithful. I can obviously look back and realize how foolish and naïve I was, but in some weird way, creating and believing that separation could be possible made me feel better. Maybe it was like I had my own set of armor to protect me when I was able to be seen by others. I could maintain an image of myself I wanted others to witness, and I had gotten pretty good at it. Except, when I took that armor off in my own privacy, I felt like I was going into a battle unprotected but at least I was the only one that could be harmed.

Over time, I noticed that my so-called armor was beginning to crack. I noticed my own negative feelings when I was in high school, and throughout my college years and beyond, signs of something deeper would pop up more often. The frequency of how I spoke unkindly to myself did not concern me until I started having panic attacks and intense episodes of depression on a daily basis. I find that trying to explain a panic attack to a person who has not experienced one firsthand is often difficult. If you have experienced a panic attack, then you will understand what I mean when I say that even taking your next breath feels like hard work. My panic attacks often start with physical sensations I can feel immediately as my skin becomes a little warmer in my face. I feel my heart begin to race, and my breathing becomes shallow. It feels like I've lost control of my own body as it goes into paralysis mode, and that is typically when the ugly crying begins. Everything about a panic attack is uncomfortable. After I had a panic attack, I would feel embarrassed, guilty, and ashamed because I lost control and could not keep it together. I do not want anyone to witness this side of me, so I did my best to keep this side of me hidden.

Specifically, I remember when one of my roommates in seminary witnessed this dichotomy. I would be fine during class but then go back to the apartment to shut myself off from everyone and everything. Truly, it would be night and day as I would socialize and put on my best face when I was out in public, and then go back to our apartment to sulk in my room. I barely ate and sleeping always felt like a nightmare. Then I'd wake up the next morning feeling exhausted as if the sleep I had was useless. I did my best to not let her, or others see that I was struggling. She was one the first people who started to see through the cracks of my person and that made me feel even more embarrassed and ashamed that I was a grown adult who had no idea how to process my own feelings and emotions productively.

If a baby cries or throws a tantrum, we accept it for what it is. A baby has no other way of communicating its needs, so the norm is that babies are socially allowed to have a full breakdown in public. If a grown adult throws a tantrum or has a complete meltdown in a public place, we would move as far away from that scene as possible because of the intense level of discomfort we would feel. Perhaps nowadays, we would whip out our phones to record the breakdown and put it on the internet to further communicate how socially insane, inappropriate, and unacceptable it is for a grown adult to lose control of themselves. Thankfully, my roommate never broadcasted or advertised that I was one person at our apartment and another person in the classroom, but I have no doubt I had unintentionally put a large barrier between the two of us.

My second semester of seminary took place at the start of 2020, which many of us know was a time that the whole world changed. The few relationships I had in this place took an immediate halt, and my spiritual life seemed to mirror the reality that life as we all knew it shifted entirely. The loneliness I felt increased, I was having panic attacks a few days out of the week, and my depression hung over me constantly. Needless to say, that internal dialogue I mentioned earlier had a field day as my mental and emotional health declined. I reached a new point in my journey as everything felt unknown. How long would we have to stay inside? How long do I have to attend virtual classes? Will I still be able to keep my part-time job to make rent this month? Is God witnessing the same things as me? Does God hear the prayers of my own suffering and pain?

Many of these questions did not yield an immediate answer, and instead, the whole world was left to sit in this liminal space as media and news sources tried to keep telling us we're living in a "new normal" whatever that was supposed to mean. As mortified as I was at my roommate witnessing my panic attacks, I discovered that there is something far worse than feeling out of control with my emotions. I walked through a scary experience of apathy and numbness. Prior to the pandemic, I recognized my emotional and mental health were both all over the place. And even during a panic attack I still felt sensations in my body and thoughts in my mind. In those moments, I was reminded that I could still feel something even in a setting that felt stagnant. But as the pandemic went on, I slowly convinced myself that it was better to feel absolutely nothing than to feel anything remotely uncomfortable. This season of my life is one where I look back and realize what a shell of a human I was. I completed the necessary tasks I needed to, but my heart wasn't in anything. I had already been good at distancing myself off from people on my own terms, but when the world took that perceived level of control away from me, I shut down completely. Many days began with a question as to why I'm doing what I'm doing, and I couldn't seem to find an answer. Eventually, the self-reflection turned off as I told myself it's better to hit the snooze button, sleep longer, and then stare at the ceiling of my own dark room as the world and all its vibrancy dulled.

To this day, one of my biggest fears is going back to feelings of apathy and numbness. At least if I'm angry, I still feel something. At least if I'm sad, then my heart still aches for something. But this season was nothing. My own apathy transformed into a new kind of self-loathing that still makes me emotional. How could a God that we declare is good, comforting, and holy allow one of His children to despise who they are? The words I said to myself paired with a world event that had no end in sight made it easy for the harsh words to penetrate my mind and heart to where I did not recognize myself anymore. The scariest part was that I really reached a point where I thought the world wouldn't know if I wasn't there. I started to think that life simply was not worth living.

I'd like to take a brief moment to speak to the realities that some people know better than others when it comes to thoughts of suicide or self-harm. While I have never acted upon my own de-structive thoughts, it does not make the feelings of those thoughts any less significant. If you're a person who struggles with thoughts of self-harm, harming others, or suicide, it is not a sign of weak-ness to ask for help. These are the parts of life and our own hu-manity that need more attention and care. I've heard numerous stories of people who lost family members or friends to suicide, and the aftermath that communities and families are left to nav-igate are incredibly challenging. It's always unfortunate when a person says, "I did not even know *insert person's name here*, felt that way because he/she/they never mentioned it. They always seemed so happy." There are a myriad of resources available to help cope with these realities, but it is scary to take those steps because it means admitting that something is not okay. It means being vul-nerable with other people and letting them see the not so good parts of us. It means admitting to ourselves that we need others to help us get through the dark night of the soul.

According to the American Foundation for Suicide Prevention, suicide is the 12th leading cause of death in the United States.[24] In 2020 alone, nearly 46,000 Americans died by suicide and there were an estimated 1.2 million suicide attempts in the same year.[25] The harsh reality of those statistics is that the numbers are probably much larger because many accounts of suicide or attempted suicide go unreported. According to the CDC, "youth and young adults, ages 10-24, account for a [whopping] 14% of all suicides."[26] To my surprise, adults aged 35-64 account for 42.7% of all suicides in the United States.[27]

I grew up in a context where things like depression, anxiety, panic attacks, and thoughts of self-harm or suicide were too taboo to discuss. I have experience with people in my life who express the same sentiments I felt that life is not worth living. It's an incredibly scary thought to have, and I wonder how many people could actually form a community and have solidarity with each other if we were willing to pay more attention and listen to our friends and loved ones who express they are hurting. Often, I hear the narratives that we need to "pick ourselves up by our bootstraps," or we simply need to "buck up." In the church those phrases sound more like, "You should pray about it and then everything will be okay," or "Don't worry. God has a plan, so everything will turn out okay." Seldom do these phrases bring comfort, and it honestly says more about the person saying them than it does about the person who is suffering. I think the last thing a person who is suffering wants to hear is that their pain, sorrow, sadness, and suffering are part of a divine plan. These phrases we tell ourselves or others are more destructive than helpful because it reveals that we as a society and culture have silently agreed that addressing anything related to pain or suffering should be dismissed and not discussed. It says that we are so uncomfortable with a significant experience of being human that we would rather put a small bandage over a

24   https://afsp.org/suicide-statistics/
25   https://afsp.org/suicide-statistics/
26   https://www.cdc.gov/suicide/facts/disparities-in-suicide.html
27   https://www.cdc.gov/suicide/facts/disparities-in-suicide.html

bone-penetrating kind of injury. I'm here to say that if you're suffering from an injury where a bone is protruding, a Band-Aid will not fix that serious of a wound.

I'm ready to see a world and a Christian culture that looks more like Jesus Christ. I'm ready to see a community of people who depend on one another and are not afraid to ask others for help, resources, or even rescue. Why is it that it takes something as drastic as tragedy or full natural disaster for communities to finally start acting like communities? Christ moved towards suffering to offer restoration. He moved towards brokenness to offer healing. He moved towards sorrow to offer joy. And he moved towards death to offer life. One of the most profound things Jesus Christ demonstrated throughout the gospels is his ability to listen and ask questions. He rarely tried to fix the problem by telling a person what he would do, and he never once dismissed a person with a Christian-like phrase that did more harm than good. I think what Jesus displays to the woman at the well, the blind man, the hungry crowd, the fatigued disciples, and many more is an inclination and preference towards holy listening and wholly listening.

Throughout the New Testament reader's witness a variety of relationships where one person guides another spiritually. We read how John the Baptist prepares a way for Christ to come and tells others to be ready. The Apostle Paul writes epistles to the churches in various places exhorting, admonishing, correcting, and rejoicing with the recipients of the letters. In the gospels, Christ continuously guides individuals, crowds, and the disciples to look closer to see the work of God the Father in their own time in history. For the postmodern church and community of Christians, the ancient practice of spiritual direction grows and flourishes to offer space for people to do the same – to take a closer look and see how God continues to work and move in our space here and now.

I became acquainted with spiritual direction in my second semester of seminary when the world began to shift, and my mental and emotional health held a tight grip of control over how I saw myself. It started with a simple request from a peer who was in his second semester of the spiritual direction program the seminary offered. He admitted that he was still learning himself and that he needed to offer spiritual direction sessions per the curriculum of the course. He told me that spiritual direction sessions are very much like conversations between two people where one person, the director, asks questions to the other person, the directee, in hopes that together the two can bear witness to the work, activity, and movement of the Holy Spirit in the life of the directee. I figured I did not have much to lose, and if I could help out a friend that only took an hour of my time, why would I not? What preceded, in the sessions I had with him as my director, completely altered how I understood the Triune God and how I understood myself.

At first, spiritual direction seemed like counseling or therapy. I spent an hour in conversation with my friend who mainly asked questions and would give a few comments here and there. One observation from our first session was that it felt nice to finally have a space where I could talk about something in my life without someone immediately trying to offer me a possible solution or quick fix. The atmosphere of the sessions was warm and inviting. Even though my director said that he was still learning, it felt like he knew exactly what he was doing, which really says a lot about his own pastoral heart. If I said something I thought was controversial, he never corrected me or tried to argue against my assertion. When it felt like the conversation was moving in a direction I was not comfortable with, he did not push me too far to a breaking point. He sat with me, listened, and asked intentional questions. He gave space for my emotions and feelings to be held, he offered consolation when necessary, and pressed into things he felt the Spirit calling him to explore and consider more deeply.

Alice Fryling describes spiritual direction as "a way of companioning people as they seek to look closely, through the eyes of their hearts, at the guidance and transforming work of God in their lives."[28] In other words, a spiritual direction relationship is

---

28   Alice Fryling *Seeking God Together.* (Downers Grove, IL: IVP, 2008), 11.

one where the people involved are invited and welcomed to actively participate in the shared work for themselves that is manifested from God, Christ and the Holy Spirit. I arrived at my sessions as imperfect, sinful, and worthy of being condemned and judged. What my spiritual director offered in our sessions was space for me to arrive as my whole, authentic, imperfect self, and be heard and told that the Triune God cares for me deeply. Throughout the gospels, Christ is seen as the figure who listens sincerely, who feels deeply with those seeking his help, and proclaiming the work of God the Father in the realm of humanity. Like Christ does for us daily, my director chose to listen carefully to my words, to offer words of comfort when needed, and to ask questions that pointed me and directed my attention to the truth of who God reveals himself to me.

Spiritual direction finally gave me words and ways to navigate conversations that were vulnerable and raw. Much of life is actually more of those vulnerable and raw moments than we lead others to believe. I remember having one spiritual direction session where I served as the director, and my directee was a person who I thought had it all put together. This person had a social media presence that looked fabulous, and it seemed like blessings continued to fall into this person's lap. And yet, I discovered through our sessions that person was aching more than I realized. That person had constructed a type of persona that others were meant to see, and our sessions together revealed the simple fact that there was so much more lying beneath the surface. Spiritual direction offers these holy spaces for people to be invited to further explore what God is actively doing in their lives. Maybe that looks like an answered prayer we did not recognize at first. Other times it is a simple space that says, "God understands your struggles, and God cares for you deeply." What a blessing it is to be reminded that God cares about the most extravagant, glamorous parts of our lives just as much as the miniscule, monotonous parts too. God witnesses our greatest victories and our deepest sins. Spiritual di-

rection gave me a home to have these realizations and to connect
back with my Creator and my own humanity.

In one spiritual direction session, I remember my director
asking me if he could read Psalm 13 and I said he could. Psalm
13 says this:

> [1]How long, O Lord? Will you forget me forever? How
> long will you hide your face from me? [2]How long must I bear
> pain in my soul, and have sorrow in my heart all day long?
> How long shall my enemy be exalted over me? [3]Consider
> and answer me, O Lord my God! Give light to my eyes, or I
> will sleep the sleep of death, [4]And my enemy will say, "I have
> prevailed;" my foes will rejoice because I am shaken. [5]But I
> trusted in your steadfast love; my heart shall rejoice in your
> salvation. [6]I will sing to the Lord, because he has dealt boun-
> tifully with me.

I feel like the Psalms have the reputation of being joyful.
Many people cite the psalms for things such as rejoicing gladly,
singing songs, playing instruments, and proclaiming the abundant
love of God. All of those things are definitely found in the Psalms.
What we see here is one of a handful of psalms that I think speak
to the other reality of life – that there is suffering and feelings of
God's silence or abandonment. I want to be clear and say that God
did not abandon me in my season of distress. In the same way, the
Israelites cried out for God as they wandered in exile. God still
remained with them there. I felt like Psalm 13 was so fitting for
the things I had brought that day to a spiritual direction session,
and when I experience seasons of transition or poor mental and
emotional health, I am reminded that I too can cry out like the
Psalmist. I am allowed to have those feelings and declare where
the Lord has gone. I am allowed to fully express the emotions
others would deem as "negative" or "unappealing" and question
how long my enemy will be exalted over me. I am allowed to beg
for God to open my eyes to see the light in the darkness and be re-

minded that the Lord's steadfast love remains. Psalm 13 is a psalm that conveys the reality that humanity is messy.

I distinctly remember a spiritual direction session I had where my mental health was on a downward spiral. I felt completely stressed and overwhelmed while also feeling incredibly apathetic and hopeless. This, my friends, is a horrible way to live and I hope you do not experience that dichotomy. My director continued to ask questions that centered on my prayer life. I admitted that I had not been praying that much because I honestly was not quite sure how to pray anymore. It was a season where it felt like God was so far away, and when I did pray it felt more like my prayers were going into a bottomless abyss rather than directly to the creator of the universe. Regardless of how I felt about prayer in that session, my director did something I was not expecting. He told me that if I felt comfortable with it, he wanted me to use the next few moments to pray to God out loud. He assured me that he would be silent in those moments and be more like a comforting presence than a guiding force. I told him I was willing to try it and so we began. This was one of the most meaningful experiences I ever had in spiritual direction, and to be honest, it was one large reason why I chose to explore the practice of spiritual direction more intentionally.

My prayer for the first time in a while was honest. At first, I was not sure what to say, and so I told God that I was not sure where to begin and that it felt like I forgot how to talk to God. I told God I was not sure if he was still listening to me. I told God that it felt like I could not feel the presence of the Spirit anymore. I apologized for the ways in which I had behaved, and that through my apathy I discovered that I purposely distanced myself from the gift of transformation. I apologized for the ways in which I had not been a faithful servant and that at times I was not even sure what I was supposed to be working towards anymore. I asked God for forgiveness for the ways that I spoke to myself. I asked God to forgive the destructive words I started to believe. I prayed that God would forgive the way I had treated others and

blamed my own mental health for my actions. At this point I had
been crying quietly, and before I continued, I took a deep breath.
I asked God to show me what transformation could look like for
me and that God would open my heart to receive such a thing. I
prayed that God would take the harsh criticism and change it into
something worthy of my own humanity. I prayed that I could give
myself permission to be made into something. I thanked God for
the ways in which he continued to work in my life, even when I
did not notice it. I took another deep breath, and said, "amen."

My director allowed space for more silence. Moments passed
where it finally felt like I could feel my soul again after a season
of feeling more like a shell of a human than an actual person. My
director simply asked, "What was that like for you?" Friends, this
is what the life, witness, and ministry of Jesus Christ is like. Jesus
Christ asked his listeners questions in order for them to see the
deeper reality of the work of the Triune God in their lives and
beyond. I looked back at an old journal entry, and it said this:
"What makes God sad is not the obstacles from his enemies, but
the rejection of his children. Our greatest call is to be transformed
by the caring love of Jesus Christ, the one whose kingdom has
already prevailed." My spiritual director did not nitpick the things
I exposed in my prayer; he simply asked what that experience was
like for me. That day, I was reminded that Jesus Christ does the
same. I was able to see again that Christ does not criticize the
things I pray about, but instead leans into the conversation deeper
and asks questions to gain more insight. God reads between the
lines of our prayers and sees straight to hearts to witness the pain
that we endure. Spiritual direction gave a place for my heart to
dwell again. I was reminded that even in those messy parts of life
– the depression, the anxiety, the thoughts of self-harm, and the
thoughts where it feels like life is not worth living and nothing is
worth my own humanity – God, Christ, and the Holy Spirit are
right there too. The Triune God steps into the messiness of life,
becomes desecrated and dirty, and is put to death in order for all

parts of life, both the tangible and intangible, to be redeemed and restored.

If you are reading this, I hope you know that the God who is the same yesterday, today, and tomorrow cares deeply for you. I hope you know that those holy spaces, like the ones I had with my director, are within your grasp too if you are willing to take a seat at the table. At its core, spiritual direction is about listening to the needs of others with a sincere posture in the same way Christ did for so many in scripture. Spiritual direction is holy listening and wholly listening.

One of the best things I gain from Psalm 13 is that God can handle my emotions, my dark seasons, and my complaints. Sometimes I wonder how often we fool ourselves into thinking God does not want to engage with our humanity. I think we do ourselves a great disservice when we try to withhold things from God that he knows more intimately and more deeply than we will ever fathom. One thing we can do is give our whole selves over to God. God created us to be whole, to be psychosomatic beings, and this includes the fact that our whole selves are broken. And in our brokenness, the Triune God moves closer to us to offer healing, transformation, and flourishing.

I challenge you to allow yourself to be fully transparent with God. May you be able to experience the gift of holy listening as you open yourself to vulnerable conversations. May you be able to extend the gift of wholly listening to another person without judgment or an agenda to fix their problems. May you practice the gift of recapturing your own humanity and feel your soul again.

Practice: Holy Listening and Wholly Listening

For this practice, consider inviting your best friend, your partner, or someone whom you feel you have an intimate connection. You might even begin by imagining yourself sitting beside someone who you feel completely loved by whether alive in this life or have transitioned. If you do this with another person present, simply ask for them to sit with you and be present. Take a few deep breaths, releasing any tension and allowing yourself to ease and settle into this space. When you are ready to begin, speak out loud to God. You might begin by saying "I don't know what to say," or "It's been awhile," or "I'm not sure you are listening, but…" Allow whatever bubbles up to come out of your mouth. If you begin to feel angry, let God hear you scream. If tears well up in your eyes, let them flow. If you feel nothing, share it with God.

When you sense you have said all that you need, take a deep inhale, then exhale and say, "Lord, I give this all to you." Repeat this for as many times as you need. End by saying, "Amen."

At this point, the practice can be officially over, but if you are with another person consider talking through what you felt in those moments. The other person should listen intentionally and ask questions for further consideration. If the other person does not have anything to ask, consider closing the time out with a shared, collective prayer.

Listening in this way might be new to a person. If you find you don't feel comfortable doing this practice with a person you know, I'd like to make myself available to anyone wanting to explore this practice. And if you discover that you'd like to experience and learn more about spiritual direction, I am a certified spiritual director, and I would like to make myself available to you.

Andre G Brown is a performer, educator and director who has been creating original theatre, music and media for over 15 years. He is a proud member of Actors' Equity and is a devoted theatre teaching artist and public-school teacher. His mission has been to bring quality arts educational programs and professional opportunities to under-served communities of color. As a professional actor, Andre has performed in national tours (in the US and abroad), regional commercials and major motion pictures. To date, he's written, produced & performed three (3) solo one act plays for public performance. Andre also holds graduate degrees from New York University & University of Washington in Acting Performance and Theatre Education. Andre is currently based in Los Angeles, CA and is producing his first documentary film, A Soul Cleansing. @asoulcleansing

For this project, Andre will be writing on Psalm 27, "From Fear to Faith: Finding Home Again."

Chapter 5

Andre Brown

From Fear to Faith: Finding Home Again

Psalm 27 (NLT)

A psalm of David.

1 The LORD is my light and my salvation—
   so why should I be afraid?
The LORD is my fortress, protecting me from danger,
   so why should I tremble?
2 When evil people come to devour me,
   when my enemies and foes attack me,
   they will stumble and fall.
3 Though a mighty army surrounds me,
   my heart will not be afraid.
Even if I am attacked,
   I will remain confident.
4 The one thing I ask of the LORD—
   the thing I seek most—
is to live in the house of the LORD all the days of my life,
   delighting in the LORD's perfections
   and meditating in his Temple.
5 For he will conceal me there when troubles come;
   he will hide me in his sanctuary.

He will place me out of reach on a high rock.

⁶ Then I will hold my head high
above my enemies who surround me.
At his sanctuary I will offer sacrifices with shouts of joy,
singing and praising the LORD with music.

⁷ Hear me as I pray, O LORD.
Be merciful and answer me!

⁸ My heart has heard you say, "Come and talk with me."
And my heart responds, "LORD, I am coming."

⁹ Do not turn your back on me.
Do not reject your servant in anger.
You have always been my helper.
Don't leave me now; don't abandon me,
O God of my salvation!

¹⁰ Even if my father and mother abandon me,
the LORD will hold me close.

¹¹ Teach me how to live, O LORD.
Lead me along the right path,
for my enemies are waiting for me.

¹² Do not let me fall into their hands.
For they accuse me of things I've never done;
with every breath they threaten me with violence.

¹³ Yet I am confident I will see the LORD's goodness
while I am here in the land of the living.

¹⁴ Wait patiently for the LORD.
Be brave and courageous.
Yes, wait patiently for the LORD.

There's something about the hottest sunlight pushing through the stained-glass window. The brilliant radiant colors cast onto the crimson carpeted pews. High-noon on any given Sunday at Ebenezer Baptist Church, in the shadows of the bustling college town of Rutgers University, there stood a 125 year old brick face church on the corner of Lee and

Comstock. There you'd see Sister Jarmon playing that Hammond B3 organ like a big old truck. With her left hand on the keys and her right hand waving powerfully pushing the choir to belt a little louder. The Holy Ghost shouts from Sister Elaine in the choir stand mixed with a few big-mouthed deacons, turned a quiet conservative Baptist church into a Pentecostal tent revival. We'd sing this one song every Sunday morning – "I'm glad to be in the service, I'm glad to be in the service one more time…He didn't have to let me live, He didn't have to let me live, I'm so glad to be in the service one more time."

I was 16 years old and I was glad to be in church. I'd wear a nice pair of hand me down slacks from a weekend of thrift shopping with my dad. My Sunday costume: an un-ironed white dress shirt, slacks with a crease, this fancy braided leather brown belt, an old pair of my dad's dress shoes and lastly a pair of glasses that I didn't need (to make me look smart). Church was my safe space, my home. In those days, I felt like God was with me. Although I wasn't the toughest young guy, I felt like God was my bigger, stronger friend, who I could always run to for help – to right every wrong and to hold all my secrets.

As a child I was teased and harassed all the time. I was called *faggot* and *sissy* and *sweet*. The only place I felt safe enough to go to hide from the ridicule was at church. I was an outcast everywhere else it seemed. In an effort to help lessen the name-calling and bullying, my mother told my brother and sister to slap my hand down when it would rise up to avoid looking like I had a broken wrist. My mother used to hold her hand like that – and I would just copy her. My brother and sister slapping my hand down hurt far worse than any of the teasing from peers at school and in the neighborhood. I felt alone, *really* alone. My solace was music. But not necessarily pop music at the time. I mean of course, I loved Whitney Houston, Gloria Estefan, and Paula Abdul but I loved show tunes too. Musicals like Porgy and Bess, The Wiz, RENT, Grease and Ain't Misbehavin' were some of my favorites. Listening to these songs transported me to a world where having dramatic flair was accepted and appreciated. So, I'd put on my headset and listen and act out of all the characters and sing their songs, performing them in full joy directly in the mirror. I was my own audience.

My mom and dad divorced when I was 4 or 5. So I never had them both in the house at the same time from what I can remember. My dad was a full time preacher and speaker, so he was busy. My mom was a budding early 90's black businesswoman. By day, she worked as a career counselor at Rutgers University. After five, she was figuring out how to take over the world and build a small empire. She was either in class getting another degree or planning career fairs for former students or purchasing rental properties. She was always on the move. As the youngest of five, this left me alone with my thoughts and my CD Walkman. My oldest brother Terrence went to Westminster Choir College where he majored in piano and choral music. I was 12 around this time. He'd come pick me up a few times a month on the weekends to hang with him and we'd typically head to a practice room on campus and sing. He'd play and I'd sing for hours. I remember those times feeling peaceful and almost heavenly. One of our favorite songs was the chorus of Take Me Home, Country Roads. "Country Roads, take me home, to the place I belong, West Virginia, mountain mama, take me home, country roads."

My brother also was the musician and director for a music group on campus that sang contemporary gospel music. Sometimes he'd let me sing with, "Partakers of a Divine Nature." I had the best time. I'd finally get to practice all of that performing I'd done in the mirror but in front of real audiences now. I'd even been given my own solo with the group. It was Kirk Franklin's song, "Till we meet again." I remember the first time I sang it with the group – something *divine* happened. Something just connected for me. Like I realized that *this* spot felt right. Singing and helping people get to God. It all felt right. I suppose that was like *my* country road and for a brief moment, I finally felt like I was home.

I first learned of the story of David through Sunday school lessons and in sermons I heard preached. The youngest of all of Jesse's sons. I was the youngest. Always outside with the sheep. I stayed outside a lot as a kid. Rejected. That was me too. And a songwriter. I didn't just love music, but I wrote songs. Like poems, but with a melody. I'd even record them on my portable cassette tape player.

When I sang, I wouldn't feel like an outcast. When I would worship and pray I finally felt accepted. Accepted by God and approved by the people in the audience. The criticisms of not being tough enough or manly enough would fade away. I remember the preacher telling me stories of David dancing before the Lord as his clothes fell off him. About how his own family judged him, but God adored him. I remember hearing about David's father not even considering that God could use him. But through Samuel the prophet reminded us, "…man looks at the outer appearance, but God looks at the heart."

Several years ago – when I was living in Seattle we had a family meeting. I joined on *facetime*. My mom was talking about getting older and she said she wanted us all to know everything about her properties and where they were located. I was in Seattle for graduate school getting a degree in Acting. My mom said, "… and I never want any of you all to feel like you can't come home because of who you are and how you live your life." Which was a strange interjection. I thought she couldn't be talking about me. I come home every holiday and call home frequently, but I was the only one living three thousand miles away. I blurted out, interrupting, "Well, I certainly don't feel like an outcast, I'm in Seattle for graduate school," and I continued. "Also, I haven't told everyone, but I *am* gay… but that's not the reason I live here." It got super quiet. I could only see my sister Alisha and my mother's face in the camera. Alisha says, "Oh Terrence, don't cry." My mother quickly responded – "let him go, he's got to handle it." My brother and I had been so close. As a kid, a teen and an adult. He was not only my brother, but my mentor and my friend. My writing partner. He never made me feel awkward. I always felt so much love from him. and now, at this moment, he just walked away. Terrence stopped calling me. He stopped texting me. No more emails of songs. No more correspondence. At all. I reached out. I sent emails, text messages, left voicemails and heard nothing. I was heartbroken. I was crushed.

When someone you love rejects you, there is this feeling of loss. A consuming feeling of grief. It is a deep darkness. A deep void that is made only more crushing knowing that they are still alive and breathing and have chosen to be apart. My life as a Christian and a worshiper was shaped by my brother. Terrence's passion, his songs, his leading and his gift had inspired my relationship with God. Our distance had devastated me in ways that caused me to lose heart. It caused me to lose faith. I thought if my brother couldn't accept me as I am, how could I accept myself. It was like he discarded me for something I tried to change and couldn't. It felt like none of our history mattered to him.

David felt all of these feelings too. Alone. Rejected. Abandoned. Ostracized. Put out. Lonely. Afraid and lost. During this dark period I would reflect on some of our favorite songs we'd sing together. These songs talked about the presence of the Lord. David wrote songs that were affirmations of God's presence. In the midst of trial, danger, pain, confusion and trouble, God would never leave him. And that God's sanctuary would always be a refuge for him. So, although family and friends may turn their backs on me. God will never leave. I wrestled for several years feeling like who I am isn't acceptable to God. That's an indescribable pain. To not be at home in your own body. There is no greater betrayal than not accepting yourself. When I received that truth, I began to unravel the years of rejection from my peers, friends and family. I started that great journey inward. What I discovered is that much of my deep hurt was compounded because I believed that what others said about me was true. That God couldn't use me. That I couldn't be authentically myself and belong to God. I thought that God would leave me. And that simply isn't true.

God has made a promise to [all of] us. That they would never leave us or forsake us. Who can separate us from the love of Christ. The scripture tells us that nothing can separate us from God's love. Life nor death, angels or demons, present or future, or any powers neither height nor death. This promise has prompted my vow, like David, to say, one thing I desire and that I will seek after is to dwell in the house of the Lord all the days of my life.

Recently, in our family group chat, my brother has acknowledged me. He's come back around. It doesn't feel like it *was* but it's better than it's been. When we move from a fear based existence to a *faith* based life, the possibilities of love increase. Our container expands. Our ability to give and receive love is enhanced. The Broadway show "The Wiz," follows the story of Dorothy who was whisked away to the imaginary land of Oz in a tornado. Charlie Smalls' lyrics to "Home," capture what it means to come home to one's own self. "*When I think of home, I think of a place, where there's love overflowing...*" and I believe, just as David the psalmist knew, that in fact, unconditional love is the true presence of God.

There is something about the hottest sunlight pushing through the stained-glass window. The brilliant radiant colors casting onto the crimson carpeted pews and me. This is a reminder of God's love for me, that God has made a home for me and a place for me to rest.

Practice

Gratitude

Thank you for rejoicing over me with singing. Thank you for bringing me to this point in my life. Thank you for the opportunity to know you and to know myself. Thank you for my mind. Thank you for the power to create. Thank you for being surrounded by so much love, beauty and laughter. Thank you for keeping me healthy. Thank you for your divine presence. (Be inspired to write your own.)

Affirmation

I am loved. I am safe. I am whole. I am happy. I am creative. All my needs are met. I have plenty for myself and even more to give. I am healthy. I am kind. I am patient. I am loving. I give from abundance. I have more than enough. I am. (Repeat over and over)

Celebration

I sing. I rap. I dance. I write. I paint. I sculpt. I embrace. I give. I give. I give. I receive. I believe. I connect. I build. I move. I shift. I change. I make. I do. I color. I offer. I love. I bring. I show. I demonstrate. I thank. I praise. I magnify. I lift. I exalt. I draw. I honor. (Do it all)

Ngakpa Dawa Norbu (Rev. Chris Lee-Thompson) was an ordained Lutheran pastor for 36 years. He now serves the Joyful Path Meditation and Healing Center as a teacher-in-training. His mentor is the 9th Domo Geshe Rinpoche. In addition, he is a certified yoga teacher through Alignment Yoga and, with his wife, Sylvia, has published a children's book, *A Day of Lovingkindness*.

For this project, he will be writing on his transition from being in Lutheran ministry to joining a Buddhist community whose first vow focuses on refuge. His wisdom invites a new look at Psalm 46.

Chapter 6

Dawa Norbu

Refuge: Be still and know

$\mathcal{I}$ had as safe and secure and stable a childhood as you can imagine.

I was born white, male, and middle class in the Heartland of the United States. My parents were both college-educated, and we lived in a university town. There was no physical, verbal, or chemical abuse in our home. While my brothers and I didn't always get what we wanted, we always got what we needed. Although it was not idyllic, and we all rebelled in our own way, we never doubted our parents' love for us.

The outside world was not without its issues. When I was small, there was the Cold War and the threat of nuclear attack. When I grew into my teens, there was the Vietnam War and social unrest. Environmental issues and the preservation of life on earth were just coming into view. While these were certainly matters of concern in our house, they seemed distant enough not to cause more than a small tremor.

In church, we sang, "A Mighty Fortress is our God," Martin Luther's great hymn, on a regular basis. Based on Psalm 46, it is a powerful declaration of God's strength in the face of the worst threats – "A mighty fortress is our God, a bulwark never failing; our helper, he amid the flood of mortal ills prevailing." Yet, while we Lutherans sang the hymn with gusto, I don't remember the issue of refuge coming up in sermons (to be honest, I don't remember sermons at all), in Sunday School, in confirmation, or even in home devotions.

This, however, is the primary image of refuge for Christians – a safe haven that can withstand the worst of whatever life (and the devil!) may throw at us. God is the ultimate protection for us – "The body they may kill, God's truth abideth still!" There is something greater that we may depend on, a power far beyond our own – even if the worst should happen – who will remain and withstand any threat. The power of God will win in the end. And we can, without fear, place our trust in this power.

There is another image for refuge used by Jesus, however. It is the house that is built on rock. It comes in Matthew 7, at the end of the teaching known as the Sermon on the Mount. In this sermon, Jesus has spoken of the traditional spiritual practices of fasting, generosity, and prayer. He has also taken traditional commandments and has expanded and intensified them as a way of forcing our attention inward, to the source of our actions – our hearts and minds. He is not merely upping the ante. Jesus is calling us to transformation. When he says, "Unless your righteousness exceeds that of the scribes and Pharisees, you will never enter the kingdom of heaven," he is not telling us we have to out-pharise the Pharisees, to become even stricter about our adherence to the law. Rather, according to Dallas Willard (in, The Divine Conspiracy), he is telling us to become the kind of people who naturally do what the law requires. Complete outward conformity is neither possible nor even desired. What is possible and desired is inward change.

When Jesus gets to the end of his sermon, he exhorts his listeners. "Those who hear these words of mine and put them into practice are like those who build their houses on rock. The winds blow, the storms rage, and the rivers flood, but their houses stand. However, those who hear these words of mine and do not put them into practice are like those who build their houses on sand. The winds blow, the storms rage, and the rivers flood, and those houses do not stand."

The house that is built on rock is Jesus' image of refuge. Jesus is not likening himself to a rock, a different image in faith. The rock is our transformed hearts. It is the change of character that has been brought about by putting Jesus' teachings into practice. It is this heart – shaped by the teachings of Jesus – that provides a solid foundation and, hence, a formidable refuge in every storm in life.

These images of refuge have been part of my growing up as well as my professional life as a Lutheran pastor. Whether conscious or not, they have been part of my spiritual path for as long as I can remember.

However, since retirement, I have taken another path. After years of meditating and reading, I have become a Buddhist in the Geluk tradition of Tibetan Buddhism. I have been accepted as a student by a reincarnated Tibetan lama, the 9th Domo Geshe Rinpoche. I have been ordained by her as a ngakphang, and I am now a lama (or teacher) -in-training myself. Even though I spend far more of my time studying dharma, refuge is still central to my practice. Each morning and each evening, as well as many times during the day, I take refuge in the Guru and the Three Precious Gems. While there are similarities, there are also differences.

To the idea of protection in refuge, Buddhists include the element of direction. Refuge is not only the assurance that we are ultimately safe from any danger. It is also guidance along the path. Although the idea of a guru may seem alien to many in the West, "guru" in this context essentially means, "guidance." Through this guidance, we are actively engaged and becoming better equipped to face the challenges of any threat.

The Three Precious gems – the Buddha, the Dharma, and the Sangha. These three gems are sometimes likened to the doctor, the medicine, and the nurses. The Buddha is the doctor who fully understands the truth and can properly diagnose the problem. The Dharma is the treatment for our illness and lays out the regimen for us to follow. And the Sangha – the community of practitioners

– are those who accompany us, who remind us to take our medicine, and who provide support and care for us as we heal.

It is important to remember that the Buddha became the Awakened One, because of his exploration of suffering. As a young prince, he was protected by his father, King Suddhodana, from any of the troubles of life, troubles that might inspire him to pursue a spiritual path rather than a worldly one. He gave his son the best possible life one could imagine – the tastiest food, the finest drink, the smartest teachers, the most beautiful music, the most desirable women – everything that a young man could ask for. The prince seemed well on his way to following the footsteps his father had laid out for him. He even married and had a son.

Nevertheless, Siddhartha did wander away from the palace on his own. He went out to see the world for himself. There he found, in turn, an old man, a sick man, and a dead man. Each time, he asked his servant, Channa, "What is this? What has happened? Will this happen to me?" Each time, Channa said, "Yes, aging, illness and death happen to everyone. One day, it will also happen to you."

Then Siddhartha saw a holy man, who seemed to be at complete peace. He said, in effect, "I'll have what he's having!" So, one night, he slipped out of the palace. He took off his royal robes and put on the clothes of an ascetic. He practiced privation of the physical senses to the fullest, it did not provide him what he was looking for – peace and freedom in the face of the suffering of the world.

Siddhartha then sat under a tree and vowed not to get up from that spot until he had achieved true understanding, true awakening. Thoughts and feelings came and went – some were simple and ordinary; some were extremely pleasant, and some were very fierce. Still, he did not move. He was not seduced or drawn away by pleasant feelings; he was not scared or driven off by frightening ones. Siddhartha kept his seat under the bodhi tree until he realized the truth of human suffering.

I believe that this was the question at the heart of Siddhartha's search: What causes the suffering of the world, and what can bring it to an end? This question is not unique to the Buddha. It is posed, I believe, by all the major religions. But the Buddha's answer to this question is unlike any other.

We hear this in his first teaching. After some weeks, he returned to his ascetic friends. They had rejected him when they discovered he had given into his senses. But they also saw how bright his countenance and how calm his demeanor were. They asked him what he had discovered.

Siddhartha – now the Buddha, the Awakened One – shared with them the Four Noble Truths: there is suffering; there is a cause of suffering; there is an end to suffering; there is a path to the end of suffering.

First, everyone suffers. There are no exceptions. Everyone is subject to aging, illness, and death. This may sound very depressing. In fact, in our society, we do everything we can to avoid it. In that way, we are like King Suddhodana, Prince Siddhartha's father. We try to keep suffering and thoughts about suffering as far away from us as we can. We deny it; we ignore it; we minimize it. We say, "Don't dwell on it; move on to the next thing – the next relationship, the next job, the next task." We think positive thoughts, because we don't want to think about suffering. It's a downer. And it would be – if it were not the truth – that everyone suffers. Because it is the truth, however, it is a relief. It is a relief to know that when we suffer – which inevitably we all do – we are not alone. We are not the only ones who suffer. Everyone suffers .

Next, the cause of our suffering is in our own minds. Yes, external, bodily pain is real, but it is compounded by our reaction to it. That is when it becomes suffering. This is difficult to realize. We would prefer that the cause of our suffering were located some place outside of us. Then it would be a simple matter of changing our situation – another job, another house, another car, another partner, another family. But those are only temporary solutions. The source of our suffering is in our own minds, due to our reactions and relationships to our experience – what the Buddha calls attachment and aversion.

Again, this may seem like very bad news – the problem is in me. But this is also good news. If the problem is in me, then I can do something about it. Because we can change our minds. We can work with our minds – to change the way we react to our experience, to change the way we relate to other people.

Finally, the Buddha identified the path that leads to this change. We don't have to figure it out for ourselves. The Buddha laid out the Eight-Fold Path: Right speech; Right activity; Right livelihood; Right effort; Right mindfulness; right concentration (samadhi); Right view; and Right thought.

These may seem fairly random when you first hear them, but I think it's helpful to see them in three steps. (cf. Thubten Chodron, Buddhism for Beginners, chapter 1, "The Essence of Buddhism.")

First, there is ethical discipline. Ethical discipline has to do with how we treat others in word and in deed. Using appropriate speech, practicing non-harming, and supporting ourselves with work that aligns as much as possible with our values: these are all essential to maintaining good relationships with others. What tends to get overlooked, however, is the harm that we do to ourselves when we fail to practice ethical discipline. The inner chaos that is a product of lying, cheating, stealing, and so forth, makes it nearly impossible to achieve a calm mind, which is the goal of the next step. Lying to your loved ones, cheating your customers, stealing from your neighbors are all antithetical to a calm and peaceful mind, no matter how much we might try to convince ourselves otherwise. But when we practice right speech, right activity, and right livelihood, this helps to create a mind that is more easily tamed.

This is done through the second step – meditative stabilization. We do not harm our minds in making too strong an effort, but still remain connected and engaged. We are aware and mindful of our actions, both bodily actions and mental actions, so we are not as easily driven by them. When our minds are stable, they are better focused, and we are able to see more clearly.

This clear seeing developed through a calm and concentrated mind leads to the third step, which is wisdom. Wisdom means seeing things as they really are and treating others with compassion. This happens when we realize that nothing – not even our own selves – has inherent existence, but instead is a result of a myriad of causes and conditions. This view also, however, leads to compassion – to see our own suffering, and the suffering of others, and wishing them to be free from that suffering.

This final step – realizing emptiness – is, I believe, the Buddha's unique insight among all the great spiritual teachers. Like the word, "suffering," this word, "emptiness," is another turn-off for westerners. The Sanskrit word, "shunya-ta," is often translated as, "nothingness." But shunya-ta is not void. And emptiness is not nothingness. It simply means that, yes, we exist, but we don't exist in the way we think we exist. This insight evolves from a meditation practice that is built on moral discipline.

My own meditation practice began after I had been serving as a Lutheran pastor for about 15 years. I decided it was finally time to get serious about developing a spiritual life. I had tried a few different things – daily Bible reading, prayer, journaling – but was never able to maintain them for very long. I had been reading Thomas Merton and thought maybe meditation would be right for me. I had also read in Morton Kelsey's book, *The Other Side of Silence*, that he had started meditating as a way of experiencing the things he was preaching about on Sunday morning.

So, I lit a candle, and I sat down. I didn't really know what I was doing. I tried counting my breaths, guided meditation, Centering Prayer, mindfulness, icons, chanting, and the like. I would do one for two or three months, get bored, and then try something else. But even with my first struggling attempts, I began to notice changes.

One of the things I disliked most among my pastoral duties was making hospital visits. Because I never really knew what I would find when I got there, my anxiety would skyrocket. Would there be someone there? Would they be in the room or not? How would they be feeling? Would they be deep in crisis? Or would the crisis have passed, and they were ready to go home? Would there be other people in the room – doctors, nurses, therapists, family? The uncertainties were endless.

One day, after I had started my meditation practice, I was walking through the hospital parking lot. I felt my anxiety rise. But then a voice said, "Why don't you focus on your breath?" I did, and by the time I got to the patient's room, I was ready for anything. Ever since that day, I have always loved to do hospital visits.

There was also a Sunday in which a thoughtful woman commented on my preaching for the day, "Your sermons have gotten deep." I thanked her, but said to myself, "I thought my sermons were deep!" When I got home, I asked my wife about it. She said, "Your sermons have been deep, but they've gotten deeper." I wasn't quite sure what that meant, but I knew it was connected to my meditation practice.

This was just the beginning for me of a long journey. After ten years of a variety of practices, I committed to a daily practice of Vipassana, which I also did for ten years. Along the way, I met a reincarnate Tibetan Buddhist lama – Domo Geshe Rinpoche. After I retired from professional ministry, I became one of her students.

One of the Buddhist practices I have long been doing regularly – even before I met Rinpoche – is the practice of Loving-kindness, or *metta*. It is a prayer-like meditation in which one sends good wishes, first, to oneself, to a beloved person, to a neutral person, and to a difficult person. Then the wishes are directed gradually to larger and larger groups of people until all beings are the recipient of your benevolence. Although there are different phrases one may use to express these good wishes, they often include wishes for safety, for good health, for happiness, and for ease in life. Because of my relatively safe life, I never gave much thought to the wish for safety. Then I heard someone say, "What would it be like if everyone in the world felt safe?" I realized it would be pretty amazing!

Perhaps I have overestimated the degree to which I feel safe – in difficult social situations, struggling with a hard decision, plagued with worry about one thing or another. Those are times when wishing safety for myself has its strongest effect. Then I begin to relax and open my heart. That is when I become more accessible to others and more aware of the possibilities for good.

This sense of safety not only helps us to be more loving toward others. It also helps open the door to deeper inner work. In discussing the effect that a problematic family life can have on one's karma, Rinpoche writes:

> That is why the first level of Buddhist refuge is to restore (or newly create) a firmer sense of stability and security. Even the soon-to-depart Prince Siddhartha, who had a perfect childhood, asked his overprotective father, "Can you keep me safe from death? Can you keep me safe from suffering?" His father had to admit that he could not. Buddhism explains that, no matter how wonderful our upbringing was and how close and supportive our family was, a perfect childhood is still faulty by comparison to the deep relationship with the three jewels of refuge. A perfect sense of safety does exist, and we absolutely must have this inner reliance to enter into the unknown territories of our own consciousness. (The 9th Domo Geshe Rinpoche, How to Change Your Karma, Hermitage Buddhist Publications, page 305).

The true outcome of outer refuge is inner reliance. This reliance engenders a stability that enables us to make progress toward awakening. This inward sense is what drew me more to Buddhism's understanding of refuge, but it is also expressed in this psalm for Christians.

While the opening verses of Psalm 46 depict powerful images of outer refuge, I find the true import of refuge is expressed in the words, "Be still, and know that I am God." God may be our refuge and strength, but this doesn't prevent bad things from happening to us. The worst thing to happen would be that we would lose our faith, to stop knowing God. By being still, however – trusting in divine refuge rather than our own strength – that we know God and remain in relationship with God.

So, it is these words in the psalm – Be still and know – that express for me the kind of refuge I seek as both a Christian and a Buddhist. The reassurance of these words brings a calm that allows me to see more deeply in any situation, to discern the most beneficial action, and then to take the next step on whatever path I am following.

Practice

Loving Kindness Meditation

What is Loving Kindness?

This practice comes from wisdom across multiple religious traditions about offering kindness to people who are not like you. Loving Kindness is the spirit of unconditional love that uncovers endless compassion for ourselves and others. In this meditation, we send love to ourselves, our Beloved, strangers and difficult people in equal amounts not because we expect change in them, but because we are open to seeing God/the Divine/Absolute Love/Light in them as we see it in ourselves. As a Christian, I experience this practice as a foundational piece in understanding how to develop the ability to love my neighbor as I love myself and even to follow Jesus more intimately by loving my enemy.

Begin with closing your eyes or gazing softly down. Allow the flow of the breath to soften the body and ease tension. Then, when you are ready, begin to visualize a light within you radiating from your heart space. Imagine that light growing brighter and extending to all parts of your body. Feel this light as unconditional love and compassion. Now, say these words to yourself slowly:

May I be safe.

May I be well in mind, body and spirit.

May I walk in peace.

May I be at ease with the ever changing circumstances in life. (repeat 3x's total)

Rest.

Now bring to mind an image of a loved one. See them in your mind's eye and imagine that light within you extending out towards them. Take a few breaths. Then repeat the words above 3x's then rest.

Now bring to mind an image of someone you don't know very well, someone you don't have a strong feeling about. We might call this person a stranger. Visualize them in your mind's eye and begin to send that same light from yourself towards them. Take a few breaths. Then repeat the words above 3x's and then rest.

Bring to mind an image of a challenging person. If this becomes too difficult, return to offering yourself loving kindness through visualizing the light or repeating the phrases. If you are able, begin to send the light towards this challenging person. Take a few breaths. Then repeat the words above 3x's then rest.

Bring to mind yourself, your loved one, the stranger and the challenging person. Begin to send the light towards each person in equal amounts. Take a few breaths. Then repeat the words above 1 time then rest.

Now, extend the light from this group through the place where you are meditating and into the community that you live. Imagine the light touching all living beings in these places. Take a few breaths. Then repeat the words above 1 time then rest.

Allow the light to flow from areas close to you across expanding around the world. Take a few breaths. Then repeat the words above 1 time then rest.

Imagine the light reaching all living beings in our beautiful world. Take a few breaths. Then repeat the words above 1 time then rest.

Visualize the light flowing out from our planet to all planets, all galaxies, to the known and unknown, to the seen and unseen. Take a few breaths. Then repeat the words above 1 time then rest.

There are people around the world practicing this meditation right now and sending you Loving Kindness! Take a moment to open yourself to receive loving kindness from others. When you are ready, rest.

When you are finished resting, gently bring the mind back to notice the body by making small movements like wiggling your toes or neck rolls. Open your eyes. Enjoy moving in this spirit throughout your day!

Dr. Angela Patterson is a media psychologist, writer and communicator who currently serves as the head writer and editor at Springtide Research Institute. Using her communications background, she also teaches organizational behavior and culture in the master's program for Organization Development and Leadership at Fielding Graduate University. Angela earned a doctorate in media psychology from Fielding, where she studied how media and technology affect cultural institutions. Specifically, her research focuses on how digital media affects the religious and spiritual development of adolescents and young adults. Angela also holds a master's degree in journalism from Indiana University Bloomington and a bachelor's degree in journalism from the University of Southern Mississippi. Angela lives in downtown Dallas, Texas and is a proud plant mom of two.

Chapter 7

Angela Patterson

My Body, My Home

*I*n *Dubliners*, James Joyce famously described his character Mr. Duffy as a man "who lived a short distance from his body." Until my early 30s, I was Mr. Duffy, plowing through life as a determined spirit dragging my body along for the ride.

Psychology shows us that when we perceive that our needs are not being met by our primary caregivers, we will find a way to get them filled. For many of us (especially in the United States), we learn early that our caregivers respond positively when we do things well. I wouldn't realize it until later, but my father's absence left me two paces behind the starting line, entering the world with an emotional deficit I'd begin trying to fill out of the gate. I wasn't old enough to tie my shoes when I realized that if I did well, those around me would not only approve of me, but also see me as valuable. While my mother and grandparents truly had my best interests at heart, they unknowingly supported this unspoken commitment to success, which stemmed from their own perceived inadequacies. They just wanted me to be good. So I became the best. And while achievement was praised, perfection was lauded. The glory that came from doing things right became a subconscious addiction. It was an all or nothing proposition – if I don't win, I must not be good at all. Incredibly flawed logic, I realize now, yet so many of us walk around with this same belief, trying to satiate this craving for love and attention by being number one.

And to succeed, it's best if you stay out of the emotions in your body, and stick to the knowledge in your head - emotions only get in the way of a win. To feel is dangerous. If something offends, brush it off. If it angers, shove it down. If it hurts, bury it deep. Keeping one's eye on the prize means remaining clear head-ed, but also requires disconnecting from your body and yourself. When you have a pit in your soul crying to be filled, though, this is a small price to pay.

This is especially true when achievement equals not just being the best in competition, but also being excellent in every way. Your body, your weight, your appearance, your clothing, your speech, your very being – all of it should always be aiming for ultimate perfection. We were clearly not born that way, I thought, so it was something we must strive toward. When you're a stocky kid with unruly curls in a home full of straight-haired petite women, leaving your body behind becomes much easier.

The internal body shaming started early. I entered Weight Watchers at 10 and was baptized into the Cult of Dieting so pop-ular in the early 90s. There was no such thing as too thin, and be-ing hungry became a badge of honor, especially if it meant going to the space in that strip mall every Wednesday, stepping on that scale, and having the crowd of hopeful girls and women witness you existing with one less pound of flesh. Victory! Like most girls, I wanted to be pretty. I kept my hair short and straightened out, exercised for hours a day (thanks to year-round sports involve-ment) and tried to appear confident. The irony of all this focus on external appearance is your body is not really a space you occupy, but a nuisance to be dealt with. The body becomes a burden.

By the time I graduated from high school, I was covered in trophies, plaques, certificates, ribbons. I was a varsity athlete, ac-ademic contest winner, homecoming queen, Miss CHS. Leading head first served me well. Yet, much of what I remember from those years are not coherent memories, but simple fragments of people, places, things, events – because I wasn't fully there. I recall working very hard, partying harder, and trying to ignore a growing sense of discontent. The unspoken mantra was "no feelings, just thinking". To be robotic was safer than humanity.

College is usually the place where people find their way and discover themselves in the process. That August of my freshman year I made the entire 13-hour drive with a smile plastered on my face because I finally felt free – free to move into this next chapter of my life, free to have adventures, free from family demands. Yet, what I'd find over those next four years is that I'd actually double down on disconnection. I'd continue to live in the Trojan Horse of Achievement around me I'd built up around me, safely nestled in its core. My own messy insides, however, were beginning to leak out – when it came to romantic relationships, the deep wound came alive in the form of problematic men and even worse choices. Despite the fact I knew it was dangerous to have feelings – to be in the heart too long was a sure way to get it broken – I entered a loop of toxicity it would take me years to get out of.

If all of this sounds intense, it's because it is. It takes immense effort to live this way. Yet, when you start very young, it becomes your default setting – and it's much more difficult to exist in any other way. Plus, when you've internalized that your very being is somehow not good enough, it's actually a relief to take great pains to separate your head from yourself. It becomes somewhat pleasant when you get to the point where the "someone different" you've created and you are actually the same thing – at least in your mind.

I spent many more years on autopilot – through a graduate degree, first jobs, second jobs. I found myself one day living in the ideal lifeworld I'd built for myself – wife, dog mom, suburban home owner, corporate ladder climber. I'd done everything one was supposed to do. At 30 years old, I'd wrapped myself in the American Dream.

But what at first felt like swaddling quickly became suffocation.

I knew the exact day I had to leave it all, and I had to leave alone. There was a draw, a calling, to go find my body. I started my search in a therapy session. Once a week, I'd go sit in front of a kind-faced woman not much older than me. We'd do exercises that showed me, in different forms and ways, that pretty much everything I'd done, said or chosen over my 30 short years was an effort to fill the void my father's absence had left – an abandonment wound, she called it. And then I'd spend the last 15 minutes of the session openly weeping. I did this for a year and a half.

But each week, on that second hand couch in a makeshift office, my head inched ever closer toward my body. Every a-ha moment, every realization (most of them completely mortifying), and every tear moved me slightly closer toward a person I'd long forgotten was even there. One could argue I didn't even really *know* she was there. And then the day came where my head and heart re-joined. That's when the pain started.

(I do not recommend this path, by the way. If you can avoid a traumatic divorce from your husband, living in the guest rooms of friends turned good Samaritans, leaving your six-figure corporate job with no plan and undergoing weekly therapy to uncover decades-old wounds - ALL AT ONCE - I highly suggest it. Such a drastic switch is not for the faint of heart.)

During this time of literally falling to pieces, I decided this was an ideal time to go back to church. I'd grown up in church, with a lay pastor grandfather and a grandmother, who as a soprano vocalist and pianist, made up 75 percent of the church's music department. Yet, by the time I was in high school I went to church with my friends, not out of any real desire but simply because that's what you do in West Texas. Christianity is cultural, and I took no real issue with it, mainly because I never considered it was something to be questioned. The older I got, the more performative church-going became for me, and I eventually stopped going. I hadn't set foot in one for years until I met my soon to be ex-husband, and we eventually found a Methodist church together. We rarely darkened its doorstep, but we'd made friends with the pastor, and he'd married us when the time came. So, in this season, the thought of sitting in the same space where I'd once stood in front of the altar was enough to send me over the edge. Instead, I found a non-denominational church in another area of town, one complete with a praise and worship band and a pastor in skinny jeans. I'd go week after week, and pour my shell of a self into a chair in the back of the room. I wasn't there to get involved, nor to make friends. I just cried on and off (which was becoming a theme for me) and prayed that God would show up. I honestly don't remember much of those months, but I do know that God managed to locate me in the back of that sanctuary on several occasions, sometimes in a kind word from a neighbor, more often in a word from the pastor that felt like it was just for me. It happens that way more often than not.

However, I do recall the one Sunday where God came and sat next to me. The sermon's scripture text was Psalm 139, and it didn't ring a bell at first until I saw the famous lines on the screens that flanked the stage:

> For it was you who formed my inward parts;
>   you knit me together in my mother's womb.
> I praise you, for I am fearfully and wonderfully made.
>   Wonderful are your works;
>   that I know very well.
> My frame was not hidden from you,
> when I was being made in secret,
>   intricately woven in the depths of the earth.
> Your eyes beheld my unformed substance.
> In your book were written
>   all the days that were formed for me,
>   when none of them as yet existed.

I confess – I never learned the Bible through and through. I never could recite chapter and verse. Yet, seeing those words on the display transported me back to the illustrated picture books and Bible lessons of my childhood – simple messages embedded in big drawings so little ones could understand how much God loved them. It turned out I hadn't grown up that much, and in this moment, I still needed the message made plain.

And here's what clicked: Therapy had shown me that I didn't know who I was, and I was overwhelmed with the process of finding out. Yet, verse 13 reminded me that my being was already grafted together inside me; God had carefully knitted together each of my flaws and my best attributes. God knew they were there, so there was nothing to be ashamed of. *I* was nothing to be ashamed of. However, since I'd started to shed the façade of the person I felt I should be, the thought of becoming what I wanted was overwhelming. I'd been thinking that this journey of self-discovery meant I now had to carefully curate a persona like before, but instead this time one that actually reflected me. But as we so often do, we attempt to do God's work when in reality God finished it light years before it lands on our to-do list. I didn't have to make anything. I just had to uncover what was already there. Psalm 139 didn't save my life, it just reminded me that I had one. One that was unique to me. One that was mine to discover and live out.

In the months and years since that moment, I've surrendered my desire (and sometimes plain ole need) to drive the self-discovery bus. This is a process I was never meant to drive, but to be led through. To enter the depths of myself and meet the person who lies beneath, and the God that's been sitting there the entire time waiting for all of me to arrive.

While I rediscovered many of the Psalms in that season of life, Psalm 139 was one I proverbially taped to my refrigerator door. As I continued on this new journey of what I like to call my Second Life, other pieces of the chapter rose up to meet me. When I read:

Where can I go from your spirit?
　　　　Or where can I flee from your presence?
If I ascend to heaven, you are there;
　　　　if I make my bed in Sheol, you are there.

If I take the wings of the morning
> and settle at the farthest limits of the sea,
even there your hand shall lead me,
> and your right hand shall hold me fast.

I realized God had been with me the entire time. When I was a mess. When I cried myself to sleep. All those times I pretended not to be hurt and believed what I was telling myself, because that was the only way I could hold myself together. God was there. But not just sitting next to me. God was in the depths of me. God was in my body. Because I'd learned that God was some omnipotent force among the clouds, it took a while for this concept to land. It was actually the sage words of Buddhist nun Pema Chodron that helped this to sink in. She wrote in *When Things Fall Apart*:

> Learning how to be kind to ourselves, learning how to re-spect ourselves, is important. The reason it's important is that, fundamentally, when we look into our own hearts and begin to discover what is confused and what is brilliant, what is bitter and what is sweet, it isn't just ourselves that we're discovering. We're discovering the universe. When we discover the Buddha that we are, we discover that everything and everyone is Buddha.

God hadn't been *with* me, but was *within* me this entire time. Why would I ever hate a place where God had happily chosen to dwell? As someone who'd struggled with their weight and spent most of her life scrutinizing her every fiber in photographs or what stood in front of her in the mirror, I came to the powerful realization that my body was something to be treasured, not trashed. I wasn't miraculously delivered from body shaming that day, but it gave me yet another reason to be kinder to myself, which was something that didn't come naturally. It was one more layer of shame removed.

And when those layers were removed, I started to become more curious about what lay beneath. What did it really mean to inhabit this body? I don't remember how I discovered Tara Brach, but I do recall when I read about the concept she calls "embodied presence". I heard her talk about how we humans can become disconnected from ourselves due to trauma and the impacts of our individual lives. She spoke of dissociation, and my heart sank into my stomach. I'd never known the word for it, but in a simple mention, she'd described a large swath of my life. Meditation would become a gateway to re-enter myself, body, mind and spirit. What I didn't expect was that diving into the emotional and spiritual depths would unlock physical pain. I developed terrible insomnia and woke up most mornings feeling like I'd been in a fight. Mysterious swelling, aches, pains, fatigue, ear ringing and nerve pain would place me squarely in the Medical Industrial Complex. For two years, I swam in a sea of doctors, lab work, imaging and resulting invoices only to be told that nothing was medically wrong with me. I was grateful, and it confirmed what I'd suspected – the work I'd done to re-enter my body had unearthed so many unresolved emotions (perhaps too quickly) that the overwhelm manifested as physical pain. I realized that while meditation was necessary to excavate all these buried feelings, it would take something more tactile to move them out.

I stumbled upon Elizabeth Dialto on social media, who is a self-identified healer and embodiment coach who helps women toward joy and liberation by reconnecting them to their physical selves. I listened to her talk about how each one of us is "love in a body" and I wanted to literally personify that idea. When I experienced her brand of sacred movement – a mix of free dance and movement of the hips like you'd find in salsa or bachata – my aching body creaked and jerked until it found a fluidity I'd never felt before. The music has a way of putting your mind on pause and letting your body take over, shifting how it wants to shift, releasing whatever volunteers to come forth. Moving in a way where femininity was leading the charge opened up a door of acceptance that had long been firmly shut. Part of being a child of God, a divine being, was also showing up in this world as a woman – soft and fluid, never forcing, only surrendering and moving with the currents of life. This style of embodiment helped me fully step into the fullness of myself, the "me" that God fearfully and wonderfully made.

Suffice it to say I have not arrived anywhere. I might have found my body, I may have discovered myself, but I know I'll spend the rest of my life learning who I am and who God made me to be. Yet, each month that passes, I smile at my reflection in the mirror more often. I move with less pain and more ease. I sit a little longer in the silence of meditation. It's easier to hear the still small voice from above. And I continue to sink further into my core, where the divine dwells, knowing that the hard work of reconnection is now behind me.

Practice

One of the most powerful embodiment practices I've received was given to me by my physical therapist who specializes in pelvic pain.

"Have you ever heard of diaphragmatic breathing?" she asked. "Like deep breathing?" I replied.

She shook her head and proceeded to show me a new way to filter breath in and out of my body. She told me to inhale deeply, expanding my rib cage and pushing the air deeply into my pelvis, and then on the exhale release the air as if you were tightening a corset around your core, lengthening all the surrounding muscles. I inhaled and the air made it to my breastbone at best. I looked at her quizzically, and she said to keep going. On the next inhale, I felt the air seep deeper downward, and a flash of panic ran through my body. I'd spent the majority of my life trying not to expand, not to take up space. Over the years, I trained my body to keep my head up, shoulders down and stomach tucked at all times. Before that moment, I'm not sure I'd ever really taken a truly deep breath.

It took me a few tries, but I started to get the rhythm. When I envisioned that corset tightening, I could feel all those muscles in the trunk of my body start to extend outward and straighten from the coils they'd become. I noticed my entire body start to relax, and just that moment of "undoing" caused a bit of discomfort.

I realized in that moment what a disservice I'd done to my body (and myself) over the years by doing everything in my power to keep everything small, tight and together.

Sadly, many women, especially those who were immersed in diet culture at any point, have a similar story to tell – one of deprivation that manifests in so many ways. Embodiment practices, like breathing techniques, reconnect us with our bodies in a way that allows us to take up the space we were meant to occupy. It gives us permission to notice the sensations and what emotions are tied to them. It provides a way to feel ourselves fully and holistically.

My physical therapist taught me a specific form of diaphragmatic breathing that helps to reduce pelvic pain. Yet, the practice in general works for all sorts of chronic pain or just general relaxation. The Cleveland Clinic notes that diaphragmatic breathing reduces blood pressure and heart rate and increases blood oxygen levels, and also is a tool in treating anxiety, asthma and COPD. They instruct beginners to approach the practice using the following steps:

» Lie on your back on a flat surface or in bed, with your knees bent and your head supported. You can use a pillow under your knees to support your legs.

» Place one hand on your upper chest and the other just below your rib cage. This will allow you to feel your diaphragm move as you breathe.

» Breathe in slowly through your nose so that your stomach moves out, causing your hand to rise. The hand on your chest should remain as still as possible.

» Tighten your stomach muscles, so that your stomach moves in, causing your hand to lower as you exhale through pursed lips (see "Pursed Lip Breathing Technique"). The hand on your upper chest should remain as still as possible.

Rev. Courtney Armento is driven to inspire the power of community to create systemic change, in that vein she co-authored resolution GA-1928, A Call to See and Respond to the Crisis of Domestic and Intimate Partner Violence, adopted at General Assembly 2019. Courtney is intentionally Un*Unsilencing Domestic Violence with her training curriculum.

Courtney graduated from Claremont School of Theology in 2019, with her Master of Divinity, and earned a 40-hour certificate in Domestic Violence Crisis Intervention, in 2018. She was ordained in the CC (DOC) in 2020. She earned a STAR I certificate (Strategies for Trauma and Resilience) in 2021. She is also a Midwife Pastor for theBLEND Church Family in Lancaster, California. She leads a group of impassioned pastors, called WHOLE Disciples, who collaborate on ways to bring the wider church into conversation and action around Abuse Awareness and align with GA-1928. Prior to seminary, she garnered over 20 years-experience in hospitality management, accounting management and specialized in key organizational innovation strategies for performance enhancement and risk reduction.

For this project, Courtney will be using Psalm 139 to explore God's presence.

Chapter 8

Courtney Armento

God is Here for It!

T here I was, standing on the side of the road. In front of the Whole Foods on the Near North Side of Chicago. Cars were whizzing by me as I was frozen in a trance-like state. I had locked my keys in the car for the very first time in 7 years. I'd owned this particular car for several years, and not once had I locked the keys inside, in fact I could swear there was a failsafe against locking your keys in the car that obviously did not work on that day. I dashed into Whole Foods for a quick snack. Something I felt I couldn't live without. I was on an important mission. Or so I thought.

It was January 19, 2010, I had been listening so closely to God for direction about this particular mission that I was nearly deaf and mute to all the life happening around me. I was moving in what seemed like slow motion. So slow, that I was essentially the pillar of salt. This "key" event was my cue to stop the fight. I had been in literal knots over this issue for weeks. After wasting a half a day getting the spare set of keys from my house and getting back to my car was a sign from God to me to just stop moving. But I had been hijacked. I realized that I had been hijacked by my anxiety, my mission and my need to hear from God.

Maybe you remember when our regular "free" television was hijacked under the Digital Transition and Public Safety Act of 2005, the full-power broadcasting of analog television in the

United States was hijacked. You might even remember the free TV converter box coupon program? This program was the interim conduit to television viewing during the conversion process. Those signals from the converter box were awful. Endless frozen pictures. Consistently interrupted shows. Trying to watch TV during that time was a hot mess.

Well, at that moment in January, I was a hot mess. I was full of anxiety and stress about some circumstances in my life. I was all twisted up in the game. I had intentionally silenced my world of television and the radio so I could hear from God about my next move. Folks who know me know that music is my jam and I always have music playing as the soundtrack for my life. Giving up music was a big deal. I was listening *so* hard. But I could not hear. That is when I found myself in front of Whole Foods. Frozen. Listening. Feeling as if I was in this surreal slow motion picture.

I was embroiled in a custody battle over my 16-year old daughter with my ex husband. On top of his audacity of taking my daughter, he was suing me for child support when he made 20 times more money than I did. I also still had a son to care for. Losing my daughter was devastating and added to that was the overwhelming weight of being sued for child support and it was all just enough to push me over the wild edge of anxiety.

However, I had a secret weapon against his lawsuit. The same judge that ruled in our divorce case was also the judge who would now hear the case on child support and custody. In our divorce case, my ex-husband was ordered to pay 50% of extracurricular activities and child care. Surprise! He never paid his half, and I was diligent about saving the proof of his contempt of the court's ruling. It was my smoking gun.

I was representing myself in court against his seasoned attorney and I wondered if I should file a counter suit for credit against his claim for child support from me. I was listening for God's voice or a sign from God about whether I should file or not file. My sign came as the disruption of locking the keys in my car that threw a wrench in my plan to go file the document before work. I knew something mystical was happening, I could feel it.

The next day, I went to the gym and got on a treadmill. I was still in a haze of listening. The owner of the boutique gym came up to me and offered me the remote control. I refused it. Didn't he know I didn't watch TV? Didn't he know I was waiting for a word from God? Obviously not. He offered it again. Again, I said no thank you. He offered it to me a third time. I kid you not, he tried 3 times. You know the significance of the number 3? Biblically, when something happens in 3's it is a sign that something really significant is happening. Ok fine. I took it. A southern woman pastor named Beth Moore came on and said in her southern accent. "Have any of you got you some anxious thoughts?" Whaaaaaa... I leaned in closer. She said, "our anxieties are known by God." She then went on a tangent preaching about what my life had been about for the past month. Every detail of my anxiety and thoughts of revenge and the pain of my heart was carefully and intentionally unpacked and laid bare on national TV by this Southern Pastor.

She preached on Psalm 139 "To Know and be Known." She preached on Romans 12:19-21 too.

> "Take courage my friends" she said- "revenge belongs to the Lord -" I will repay" says the Lord. Beth literally answered every question I had. I was feeling that my mission was an act of revenge, an act of retaliation. This is what Beth Moore said next:
>
> "On the contrary, "If your enemy is hungry, you feed him; if he is thirsty, you give him something to drink. And in doing this, you will heap burning coals on his head. Do not be overcome by evil, but overcome evil with good!" Overcome evil with good!
>
> God said, "Listen to me, give it to me. I esteem it. I know it. I will deal with it...." We go, "Lord, I want you to judge them but I don't only want you to judge them, I want to be able to see it...I want a front row seat." Right? Right!

Good will handle it![29]

I was on that treadmill walking and crying, crying and walking. I knew full well that day that God knew exactly what was going on in my life. I was angry, and resentful and I wanted a front row seat to see my ex husband feel my pain. I was so stressed out I couldn't see what was right in front of me. Sometimes God is subtle, and sometimes unmistakably direct. What I know for sure, is that anxiety, stress, worry and doubt, blocks the frequency, the transmitter, our very connection to God. But God has ways of getting through to us. This was my God moment!

Beth shared a story about her Bird dog that had tussled with a porcupine and had quills sticking out of her face. She said the quills have poison on the ends of them. When we have been hurt, it seems like we too have been stuck with poisonous quills and we infect others with our anger and rage.

She said her husband held her dog's face in his hands and gently pulled the quills out. She said we have to place our chins in Jesus's hands and go through the same process of liberation from hate.

Beth said we should "...give it to Him. Not just release it into oblivion. Give it to Jesus who says to us confidently, "Here's what your soul can know very well, I will deal with it -- I will deal with it." And either they'll be sorry or they'll be sorry. Do you understand what I'm saying? Either they'll come to a place in their tenderness that they're sorry or they'll be sorry. But God is the only one that can deal with that. "

I was a sobbing mess, feeling heard and held on that treadmill. I was convicted, I was reassured, I was feeling wonderfully claustrophobic wrapped in the total love and care of God. I was able to feel myself releasing the toxicity from my body.

Chile, If that wasn't enough Beth speaks with authority when she delivers this next part and I was spent.:

29   Beth Moore, "Pastor." Wednesdays With Beth, episode Week 4, Life Today, 20th January 2010.

"...Yada," that knowledge. Search me and know me; I am known. It is a word that means all of the intimacies that we think it means between us and our God but it also means, and I told you at the very beginning, it always involves acknowledgment and understanding. It means to be acknowledged and understood. I need you to know today your God acknowledges what you've been through. Part of us is just carrying it like a crusade. And what's happened to our loved one, when we just carry it like a banner before us because we want somebody to go, "Man, you've been through something awful!" We want it acknowledged! We may get that from some people but it will never be enough -- it will never be enough because they can't fix it. They can't do anything about it but God can. I want you to know, he acknowledges what you've been through. Do you hear what I'm saying to you? He knows what you've been through. He acknowledges the depths of it -- the hurt of it -- the devastation of it. He understands what makes you tick and what makes you hurt, and what makes you anxious and what makes you fearful! He gets it! The beauty of it is, he is the only one in the universe that can do anything real and lasting about it. (Beth Moore)

Beth was talking directly to me! The Show came on just when I turned the TV on after 3 invitations. Every bit of my anxiety was addressed, all of my feelings of nerves, rage and anger, all of my need for a daddy God to hold my little chin in his hands and heal me. I was infected but knew I could trust that God had witnessed and fully known my pain. I was ready to give it to Jesus and trust him to handle it for me while I heaped burning hot coals on my ex husband with glee. (Spiritual coals, I would never hurt him)

There are several instances in my life that I can point to and say - but God! Only God! That was clearly a God thing. Psalm 139 is above all, is my direct connection. It reminds me that I can trust in God. I went home that evening after the day of collecting myself and getting to work and decided to read and meditate on Psalm 139 and picked up my Bible and it fell open to Psalm 139.

This is a powerful moment from my faith journey. One of **THE** single most powerful moments, and it is my anchor to my faith.

Being anchored in the past to an experience that tethers you to your faith and reminds you of God's movement and presence in your life is the stuff that serves as a beacon to the future- you can draw on it anytime you feel unsteady or as if you need attune yourself to God for a clearer signal.

God is always speaking, we have to reduce the static to tune in. Static isn't just outside noise, our interior landscape has to be static free. Anxiety free worry free -The good news is no matter how much we scramble the frequency god can still get a broadcast through, but why go through the struggle if you don't have to?

Rev. Julian DeShazier, pastor of the University Church Chicago, calls this a "wildly claustrophobic text, about a Claustrophobic God." There's nowhere we can go to be free of God! What a deliciously captivating and reassuring concept.

There is no where you can go that God is not with you. All the days of your life are known to God, you are known by God. God knows your anxiety —-that knowledge is too wonderful! Before we speak it it is known by God.

Walter Brueggemann beautifully grounds our sensibilities within the Psalms when he suggests:

> The Psalms of orientation were created, transmitted, valued and relied upon by a community of faithful people. To these people, their faith was both important and satisfying. A beginning theological point for the Psalms are those psalms that express   a confident, serene settlement of faith issues. Some things are beyond doubt, so that one does not live and believe in the midst of overwhelming anxiety. Such a happy settlement of life's issues occurs because God is known to be reliable and trustworthy...and steak life on this particular God.[30]

30   Walter Brueggemann, *Spirituality of the Psalms* (Minneapolis: Fortress Press, 2002), 16.

Oftentimes we want a certain outcome and when we do not get that exact thing, we think God was not listening. God was ignoring us and our journey is harder because of our wanting. However, I contend that God has taken us to the point where we need to be to get the outcome we need or the lesson we need. Sometimes we have to advocate for ourselves and it's hard and it's ugly, but we are made stronger because of it. We often expect God to do it all and we miss what God is doing through us and for us to shore us up for the journey. Often we are so stressed out trying to fix things on our own or in my case stressed but listening, that we can't see the openings and offerings God Is providing. We fully miss the gifts of our claustrophobic God who's in the trenches with us.

Brueggemann continues the clarification on the power of the Psalms when he states:

> The function of this kind of psalm is theological, that is, to praise God. But such a psalm also has a *social function* of importance, It is to articulate and maintain a "sacred canopy" under which the community of faith can live out its life free from anxiety. That is, life is not simply a task to be achieved... There is a givenness to be relied on, guaranteed by none other than God. That givenness is here before us, stands over us, endures beyond us, and surrounds us behind and before.... Whenever we use Psalms, they continue to assure us of such a canopy of certainty - despite all the incongruities of life.[31]

This "sacred canopy," is what I was embracing on the tread-mill before completely understanding the depth of its power to bind me and hold me with love and provision. I felt a peace beyond comprehension because of the accuracy and intentionality of my message. It was as if God Godself was talking directly to me and that knowledge reinforced the eminence of God, the intimacy of God and the power of God in a way that I have never experienced before.

---

31   Walter Brueggemann, *Spirituality of the Psalms,* 18.

Long before I entered seminary and knew anything about a lectionary, I would pass churches and notice when their reader boards shared that the pastor would be preaching on Psalm 139. It seemed to be the only scripture that I noticed. But as I noticed it at more than one church at the same time, I thought it was a special message for me. It would be decades later when I learned about the lectionary and the reason for the synchronicity revolving around pastors preaching the same text on the same Sunday in multiple houses of worship. Today, however, I still feel that Psalm 139 is still a special message for me. I dance in my soul whenever I see or read it.

I was stopped in my tracks regarding filing a countersuit against my ex husband. God told me to be still and know that God is God. I prepared the filing, however, I held it and at the appropriate time in the court proceeding I was able to use it for credit against future child support and I was heard and all things worked out for my benefit. I had been on the wild edge of anxiety and my most intimate pain was heard and the answers came. Jesus dealt with it and I could let it go under the "sacred canopy". I learned that God is here for it. I learned that anxiety scrambles the transmission of our direct connection to God.

There is an antidote to overwhelming anxiety that fits under the canopy if we can just believe in it and embrace it. What is it that compels us to throw off faith in exchange for the comfort of the stress and anxiety we know? It is a human thing, but I offer you a spiritual touchstone to aid you in letting go of angst sooner than later.

Practice:

"Today, I invite you to feel totally wrapped in God's love. Grab a blanket and fully wrap yourself up like a burrito! Then sit and take a few breaths, noticing how the blanket feels around your body."

Psalm 139 is a conduit to God…I invite you to reread the text and see what speaks to you.

Then take a moment to scan your life for that one moment above all others that you knew only God could have been involved in your comeuppance. When you have it. Let it serve as a reminder to your soul that reinforces that God is a faithful God who is always with you and never let that memory go. You are invited to journal about it.

Psalm 139 (New Revised Standard Version)

1 O Lord, you have searched me and known me. 2You know when I sit down and when I rise up; you discern my thoughts from far away.
3 You search out my path and my lying down,
and are acquainted with all my ways.
4 Even before a word is on my tongue, O Lord,
you know it completely.
5 You hem me in, behind and before,
and lay your hand upon me.
6 Such knowledge is too wonderful for me;
it is so high that I cannot attain it.
7 Where can I go from your spirit?
Or where can I flee from your presence?
8 If I ascend to heaven, you are there; if I make my bed in Sheol, you are there.
9 If I take the wings of the morning
and settle at the farthest limits of the sea,
10 even there your hand shall lead me,
and your right hand shall hold me fast.
11 If I say, "Surely the darkness shall cover me,
and the light around me become night,"
12 even the darkness is not dark to you;
the night is as bright as the day,
for darkness is as light to you.
13 For it was you who formed my inward parts;
you knit me together in my mother's womb.

14 I praise you, for I am fearfully and wonderfully made.
Wonderful are your works;
that I know very well.
15 My frame was not hidden from you,
when I was being made in secret,
intricately woven in the depths of the earth.
16 Your eyes beheld my unformed substance.
In your book were written all the days that were formed for
me, when none of them as yet existed. 17 How weighty to
me are your thoughts, O God! How vast is the sum of them!
18I try to count them—they are more than the sand; I come
to the end—I am still with you.
19 O that you would kill the wicked, O God,
and that the bloodthirsty would depart from me— 20 those
who speak of you maliciously,
and lift themselves up against you for evil!
21 Do I not hate those who hate you, O Lord?
And do I not loathe those who rise up against you? 22I hate
them with perfect hatred;
I count them my enemies.
23 Search me, O God, and know my heart;
test me and know my thoughts.
24 See if there is any wicked way in me, and lead me in the
way everlasting.

Psalm 139 reminds us that God is Here For it! God is here
for every bit of the messiness of our lives! Not just as a spectator,
but as a lover, a knower, an active participant, a provider, a guide,
a sage, a healer, a negotiator, a builder, a way maker, a potter, a
warm winter coat or down comforter (synthetic comforter if you
are vegan) wrapping us up in love and care.

Take a moment to ground yourself in gratitude for the love
and comfort and acknowledgement of our God in your life.

Play this song "Speak Lord" by SculpturedMusic before or after your practice and dance or just open yourself up in a new way to God's voice.

Practice

Reflecting upon the scripture Psalm 139 and my experience with it, I have come to a deep sense of rest for my soul that carries me along my human journey. On my journey I have floundered in a sense of worry and fear. Fear over outcomes and fear over external impact on my life and my children's lives. I found rest in the promise that God makes thorough the words that claim, no matter where we go, God is there. God is not there as a bystander or an observer, but rather a loving presence of providence and nurture. Settling into this knowledge that is too wonderful for us to comprehend, gives me the permission to be relieved of anxiety and stress. I know that there is this Holy presence that has ways that I cannot fathom, for assuaging my stress. Becoming still to the power and the presence offers me rest and relief. Becoming still is the battle. Or maybe, the battle is, becoming aware of when we need to become still is the first step. Being mindful of our anxious thoughts and their ability to unhinge us from the sacred provision is powerful. I have been asking myself lately, what is at the root of my distress? My next question is how much does it matter in the grand scheme of this life that I am trying to find and hold joy in. Am I holding onto something too tightly? Am I showing up as the childhood me that needs something to heal an aching wound? Do I feel attacked? If and when I feel attacked, I can simply remember that God's promise is to fight my battles for me and I can allow this by inviting God into the space through prayer. I can even visualize God moving the mountains for me. I invite you to close your eyes and envision the mountains blocking your path. They may be people, institutions, policies, or a sense of overwhelm at all that lies ahead of you. However big or sense these mountains are, see them seemingly large and in charge. Now, envision a sacred loving presence sitting or standing by your side radiating glorious golden light. See the presence smile at you and tell you that you are worthy of joy and abundance of all good things. Now, say with gratitude in your heart, Loving Divine Presence, I invite you to move these mountains (you can name them if you wish). You know the pain they are causing me. Please move them so that I may have peace and rest and joy in my soul. Now say thank you for all you have done on my behalf that I know of and all the things you have done that I am unaware of. I trust you with all that blocks my path forward. I thank you for your promises of rest and peace. Thank you for your love and grace. I accept your wisdom with thanksgiving. I marvel at you. Now, see the mountains crumble to dust or move out of your way. Stay in this moment and feel the swell of ease fill your soul. See the faces or places that have held you back, simply melt into thin air. Whatever feeling you have, hold it and give thanks. Emerge from this moment believing in the Holy to follow through with the promises. Reflect on this moment any time the anxiety, stress or fear tries to bubble to the surface threatening your Joy.

Michael Esterheld is a writer, a semi-nomadic wanderer and troubadour with many years of experience in church music and music ministry, across traditions and denominations. He has, at one time or another, been an actor and a theatre teacher, a bartender and a gas station attendant, a photographer and a blogger, a secretary and a sailor. But through it all he has been a musician.

After earning his undergraduate degree in the Great Books liberal arts program at St. John's College in Annapolis, Maryland, he later completed an M.A. in Eastern Classics at the St. John's College Graduate Institute in Santa Fe, New Mexico, where his studies focused on the foundational religious, literary, and philosophical texts of India, China, and Japan.

He believes wholeheartedly in the power of songs and stories to inspire and bind us together, to bring down the walls that all too often separate and isolate us, to build stronger communities, and to keep us mindful of the fact that "the only thing that counts is faith working through love" (Galatians 5:6).

Some of his occasional musings and "dispatches from the here and now" can be found on his website, UselessOldTree.com.

Chapter 10

Michael Esterheld

'My Life Flows On in Endless Song': Music, Ministry, and a Mother's Gift of Grace

"I will sing to the Lord as long as I live;
I will sing praise to my God while I have being."

– Psalm 104:33

"For he that sings praise, not only praises, but only praises with gladness; he that sings praise, not only sings, but also loves him of whom he sings. In praise, there is the speaking forth of one confessing; in singing, the affection of one loving."

– Saint Augustine, Exposition on Psalm 73

"Do not fight to expel the darkness from the chamber of your soul. Open a tiny aperture for light to enter, and the darkness will disappear."

– Saint Porphyrios of Kavsokalyvia (1907-1991)

I inherited my love of music from both of my parents. My mom, like me, was a church musician from her youth, who sang and played the piano, and accompanied my sisters and me on everything from Bach to Broadway and hymns both old and new. My dad, meanwhile, taught me to appreciate the words, to sing them clearly so that others could understand, and to love the earthy lyrics and melodies of old folk songs accompanied by the strum of an acoustic guitar. Between the two of them, there was no way out of being a lover of music and a dweller in song.

Growing up, there was a saying I loved, attributed to Saint Augustine: "He who sings, prays twice." I've heard it's really more of a paraphrase of the quote included at the start of this chapter than anything he actually wrote, but I still hope it holds true, because we certainly loved music, and the singing in our house was constant. Over the course of my life, I haven't always been the greatest at saying my prayers, but from an early age I learned the magic and sheer exuberance of making "a joyful noise unto the Lord" (Psalm 100:1), and those joyful noises – so often proclaimed in song, whether at home or at church – have been the bedrock of my faith from my earliest years.

I still remember when I was a kid, long before entering any kind of music ministry myself, hanging out at practices while my mom and her fellow church musicians were rehearsing for upcoming services. From my youth, I learned to recognize the changing of the liturgical seasons by whatever music she was working on — songs of joy and hopeful expectation during Advent; penitential songs of reflection, purification, and deep contrition during Lent; and exultant hymns of praise and Christ's triumph over death during the Easter season, with "Alleluias!" ringing out. You could almost mark the changing of the seasons in our house by the progression of major and minor melodies being played by my mom on the family piano — an old Wurlitzer upright that my parents moved, with the help of some friends, through an apartment window at the start of their marriage. That's how precious that piano was to my mother, and how important to them both it was to have a home filled with music and song.

It was my mom who first taught me what it meant to be a church musician – all the joys and the sorrows inherent in the calling. She emphasized the importance of doing the best job you could while never trying to draw too much attention to yourself. It's another idea that has connections to the writing of Augustine, who loved music dearly but who was also suspicious of its raw potency and its ability to overpower us emotionally.

I remember being taught the idea that church music, while wonderful, can distract from worship not just by being bad, but also by being "too good" — by drawing too much attention to itself, or by being overly performative and showy. In a sense, it was about finding the musical Middle Way, where the music contributed and elevated the proceedings without becoming itself the focus of attention. I learned that if, at the end of services, too many people were consistently praising you as a musician, you might be missing the mark. As John the Baptist put it so succinctly, "He must increase, but I must decrease" (John 3:30). My mom drove home the point that the goal was never supposed to be to impress people, but to point them towards God and foster an experience of genuine worship through our contributions in song.

We threaded the needle as carefully as we could. At church, it was hymns and spiritual songs, and we did our best to keep any prideful tendencies mostly in check. But we were also a theatrical family – lovers of drama and the stage – and throughout my adolescence and young adult years I was heavily involved in the theatre, performing roles onstage in dozens of plays and musicals.

Jimmy Buffett, that irreverent lapsed Catholic, street corner sage, and modern troubadour, once said, "There is a deadline between Saturday night and Sunday morning." I know I felt that deadline – that threshold – palpably in the relationship between my life as a young actor and performer, and my life in church music ministry.

To be clear, even to this day I can't see how one could have been without the other. The theatre taught me to hone my artistic skills, to treat diction and delivery, vocal technique and the arts of performance as seriously as the grave. It taught me to approach everything beautiful and wondrous in life as craft, as mystery, as poetry unfolding. Meanwhile, my experiences as a young church musician taught me always to be on the lookout for the sacred, for liminal spaces, and to stand as a witness to the sacramental workings of faith, hope, and love in the human heart – both in the music I made, and in the world around me.

> "If I speak in the tongues of humans and of angels but do
> not have love, I am a noisy gong or a clanging cymbal. And if
> I have prophetic powers and understand all mysteries and all
> knowledge and if I have all faith so as to remove mountains,
> but do not have love, I am nothing." (1 Corinthians 1:13)

It's an extraordinary thing, when you think about it, to be entrusted with such mysteries – such ministries – and with such responsibilities as these. In Old Testament times, according to some mystical Jewish traditions, the high priest would wear a cord tied around his ankle when entering the Holy of Holies on the Day of Atonement, lest he be struck dead and need to have his lifeless body pulled out by the attendants, who themselves were not permitted to enter that most sacred of spaces.

The relationship offered to us under the New Covenant in Christ would seem to be a much more personal one – much more tender and immediate – but it is still and ever "a fearful thing to fall into the hands of the living God" (Hebrews 10:31). And if I'm honest, there were Sundays when I wondered whether I was really worthy to stand up there in front of the congregation, to crack open the hymnal, and to raise my voice in songs of praise and thanksgiving. I wondered whether I had enough faith and love in my heart to make an appropriately joyful noise unto the Lord and still escape His dread judgment and opprobrium.

Through it all, my mom was a rock, who I could always call on for advice, guidance, and reassurance. Until the day came when I couldn't.

> The thread in the hand of a kind mother
> Is the coat on the wanderer's back.

Before he left she stitched it close
In secret fear that he would be slow to return.
Who will say that the inch of grass in his heart
Is gratitude enough for all the sunshine of spring?

— "Wanderer's Song" by Mèng Jiaō (751-814)
(transl. by A.C. Graham)

I lost my mom a few years ago now. She died in the spring-
time, in that bright morning season — right on the cusp of Easter,
with the paschal mystery hanging like a mist in the air. After she
passed, my dad and my sisters and I spent the remainder of Holy
Week planning and preparing the details of her funeral, contemplating the mystery of her death right alongside the mystery of
Christ's own crucifixion, descent into Hades, and glorious third-
day resurrection.

Over the course of the last years of her life — through her
battle with breast cancer, her long road through chemotherapy
and recovery from surgery, and later through the kidney failure
that ultimately took her from us — I found myself, somewhat
unexpectedly, working in music ministry at a small Disciples of
Christ church in Houston, Texas. The church had a century-long
history and deep connections to my wife's family, to her grandmother and to her parents. Although it wasn't my own church,
there was a richness and a depth there, and a sense of being connected to forebears and ancestors. There was lineage and memory
in the sanctuary walls, and a living presence of those gone before,
both the known and the unknown, that great cloud of witnesses.

There were many Sundays when, even before my mom passed
away, I felt like I was channeling her and the various threads of
music and ministry woven throughout her life. She had converted
to Catholicism after marrying my dad, but her musical and spiritual roots were in the Baptist and other Protestant churches of
the South, in small-town Georgia and Alabama, where growing

up she sang in choirs and played the piano – not to mention the organ and even the accordion – just as I would years later.

So there I found myself at that old church in Houston, each Sunday morning, singing many of the same old hymns she had sung as a girl growing up years before. "His Eye Is On the Sparrow," "In the Sweet By and By," "How Great Thou Art," "Be Thou My Vision," "Amazing Grace," and a particular family favorite with roots in both Christian hymnody and the American folk music revival of the mid-20th century, "How Can I Keep From Singing?"

> My life flows on in endless song
> Above earth's lamentations
> I hear the real though far-off hymn
> That hails a new creation
>
> No storm can shake my inmost calm
> While to that rock I'm clinging
> Since Love is lord of Heaven and Earth
> How can I keep from singing?

The words of that hymn probably express, as well as anything ever could, the way that music ran like a river of praise and joy throughout my mother's entire life. Even at her bedside in the hospital, during those last few days and nights as we kept vigil with her, I remember singing together with my sisters some of the old songs we all knew, doing our best to remember the harmonies and the words to all the verses.

Later, feeling all but helpless, sitting alone by my mom's bedside while keeping one of the final overnight watches, I talked to her, read her a few short stories and essays about good Southern cooking and the warm embrace of family and faith, and sang to her some more. By that point she gave little sign of hearing or responding to us, but after a lifetime filled with praise and prayer and music, how could I stay silent during her final hours? What could I do but sing her onwards – from glory to glory – and hope that somewhere in the darkness now enveloping her she still knew the sound of my voice, and knew how much I loved her, and how much I would miss her when she was gone.

> Finally, brethren, whatsoever things are true, whatsoever things are honest, whatsoever things are just, whatsoever things are pure, whatsoever things are lovely, whatsoever things are of good report; if there be any virtue, and if there be any praise, think on these things. (Philippians 4:8)

The late Irish poet and philosopher John O'Donohue, in one of his final interviews, said that "music is what language would love to be if it could." In some ways, I feel like I've spent far too much of my own life trying to express in words what can only be perfectly said in stillness and silence – or perhaps in music, that one perfect meeting point between sound and silence, where death is powerless and life hums and thrives, and everything that separates us from one another – and from everything else that is – evanesces until we all dwell together in unity and harmony at last.

We like to imagine ourselves mustering up the courage in advance of facing the big challenges and changes in our lives. But oftentimes, that's just not the way it works — the breakup or the divorce comes seemingly out of nowhere, the job loss is sudden and unexpected, a major illness rears its head, or the death of a loved one comes too soon, and the unknowability of life swallows us up as we enter yet another season in the Valley of the Shadow.

I had a college professor who, when he couldn't sleep at night, would recite passages from Shakespeare that he had memorized over many, many years. It was, in part, a memory-strengthening technique and a bulwark against the terrible forgetting that so often comes in our later years. But he also found in those passages – visited and revisited, and reflected on over and over again during the course of his many years as a teacher at our small liberal arts college – an eternal wellspring of beauty, poetry, and human experience, wrapped up in verse and prose, to fall back on whenever life hit hard. It was the whole human experience – the transcendent and the terrible, the comic and the tragic, the mystical and the messy – all alchemized into some of the most beautiful poetry ever created in the English language.

It's a wonderful thing, to have something beautiful close at hand and ready to go, especially on the hard days. Many of us can think of favorite songs that have fulfilled a similar role in our own lives. The music might be sad or happy, joyful or full of pathos, but in times of need we cling to such music – like my professor clung to Shakespeare's poetry – like a man clinging to a life raft in a shipwreck.

For many down through millennia – including adherents of both the Jewish and Christian traditions – the Psalms have served this function. I've read that the early Desert Fathers and Mothers of Christian monasticism would often have the entire Psalter – or large portions of it – down by memory, and would chant or recite passages and verses from the Psalms to accompany their day-to-day labors, in between more formal times of communal worship. It was one way of fulfilling Saint Paul's injunction to "rejoice always" and "pray without ceasing" (1 Thessalonians 5:16-17).

In his "Letter to Marcellinus" on the interpretation of the Psalms, Saint Athanasius – writing in the fourth century – extols the virtues of every kind of biblical literature, but adds that "the Book of Psalms is like a garden," full of wonders and wisdom concerning both the truths of the Old Covenant and the promised revelation of the New. Moreover, he advises that the recitation of the Psalms offers an education both for the mind and the heart, as well as serving as a kind of mirror held up to the human soul – an image Shakespeare would no doubt approve of – through which we can deepen our understanding of ourselves and refine, day by day, our relationships, both with God and with the people around us.

Down through the centuries, believers have, to greater or lesser degrees, maintained this emphasis on the Psalter as an ancient book that also doubles as a living window into the practices of prayer, stillness, contemplation, and abandonment to divine providence that lies, however mysteriously, at the core of the Christian life.

I've heard it said that our present engagement in that life of faith – a life of prayer, fasting, and almsgiving (Matthew 6:1-18) – prepares us for the hour of our death, so that when that time comes, we might be properly disposed to accept God's ultimate invitation into everlasting life, into love and eternal communion with God and one another. From this perspective, we practice these things now, hour by hour and day by day, so that, when that time comes, we're ready to make the leap into glory.

But prayer doesn't just prepare us to die. Done well, and faithfully, I suspect it also prepares us to live, to dwell in deeper communion with God even now and to compassionately answer the many day-to-day calls to live in love and in service to those around us – to become what the clinical psychologist and St. Vladimir's Orthodox Theological Seminary professor Dr. Albert Rossi calls "a healing presence" in a broken and fallen world.

The expansive, extraordinary opening stanzas of Psalm 104 (103 by the Septuagint numbering) envelop the whole cosmos, and sing out like the overture of a great symphony.

> O Lord my God, thou art very great!
> Thou art clothed with honor and majesty,
> who coverest thyself with light as with a garment,
> who hast stretched out the heavens like a tent,
> who hast laid the beams of thy chambers on the waters,
> who makest the clouds thy chariot,
> who ridest on the wings of the wind,
> who makest the winds thy messengers,
> fire and flame thy ministers. (Psalm 104:1-4)

In a foreword to "The Psalms of David," the late Dartmouth College professor Donald Sheehan's rendering into English of the Psalter from the Septuagint Greek, University of Iowa professor Christopher Merrill writes, "The Psalms are first and foremost poems – of praise and prayer, of bewilderment and righteous indignation, of love and loss. They offer prophecies, instruction, solace, thanksgiving, testimony, history, law – in short, the full range of responses to the human condition, in the singular voice of the poet or poets known as David: the Psalmist or Psalmists who distilled the yearnings of the ancient Israelites and made of their walk in the sun one hundred and fifty poems, which form the ground of our spiritual inheritance."

I fell in love with Psalm 104 years ago while spending some time as a guest at a small Orthodox Christian monastery in the beautiful mountains and high deserts of northern New Mexico. I was a couple of years out of college, and wrestling with what seemed to me at the time to be some Pretty Big Decisions. Should I go to graduate school? Or seminary? Should I move to New York City and try to become a professional actor and musician? What about marriage and family? What kind of person did God really want me to be, and how could I remain faithful and committed to growing spiritually while living as an artist and creative person in this often-brutal, contemporary world? How would my soul survive the journey? And how was I even going to make a living or keep food on the table?

It was in this context, while spending several weeks at the monastery, that I first really fell in love with this Psalm, which in the Orthodox tradition is typically assigned to be chanted at the beginning of the evening vespers service. I would often spend part of my days working with the monks, helping them dip beeswax candles and then preparing the candles for shipment out to parish churches and other customers of the monastery. I would also spend some of my free time reading books and studying in the monastery library, or talking with the brothers or other guests, or setting off on long solo walks along the dirt roads and the trails of the surrounding canyons.

At the end of the day, though, we would gather in the small monastery chapel, light candles and oil lamps before the icons, and join in the vespers service, which begins with this beautiful

Psalm that manages somehow to tell the whole story of the creation and redemption of the world in less than five minutes.

> Thou didst set the earth on its foundations,
> so that it should never be shaken.
> Thou didst cover it with the deep as with a garment;
> The waters stood above the mountains.
> At thy rebuke they fled;
> at the sound of thy thunder they took to flight.
> The mountains rose, the valleys sank down
> to the place which thou didst appoint for them.
> Thou didst set a bound which they should not pass,
> so that they might not again cover the earth.
>
> (Psalm 104:5-9)

For me, with its mountains and meadows, its wild animals and dragons, its ships sailing out over the seas, Psalm 104 was something like a great adventure story, all about the wild beauty of the world – the beauty of being alive – and the beauty of God's extraordinary love and providence for everything that He had made. Like all great poems, it calls the reader or the hearer into a deeper experience of being alive, and into a deeper sense of purpose – to live beautifully in the world while we can; to enjoy and be thankful for the good things of life "that maketh glad the heart of man;" to go about our labors as best we can "until the evening;" and to "sing unto the Lord" through it all, for as long as we have breath in our lungs.

As I listened to this Psalm being read during those evening services, as the darkness gathered outside the chapel way out there in the desert, all my Big Decisions seemed to fall into perspective. In the end, Love was everything. Love was, in a sense, the only thing, and everything else had to follow from that, including how each of us might respond to and be taken up into the life of that Love in Christ Jesus.

I've always been a fan of epiphanies and dramatic turnabouts, but in my own life I have to admit that things seldom unfold that way. I dream of getting knocked to the ground by a blinding light, like Saul on his way to Damascus in the Book of Acts. But God usually comes into my days more like the "still, small voice" in the story of the Prophet Elijah, and all too often I'm so distracted by my worries and cares and day-to-day anxieties – to say nothing of my cell phone! – that I hardly even hear it.

I didn't leave that monastery visit with all the answers I wanted, but I did take away a renewed desire to live my life more poetically, more adventurously, and to make of it something beautiful, if I could, in whatever time God granted me. Years later, I discovered a wonderful quote from Saint Porphyrios, a 20th century Greek saint who said, "Whoever wants to become a Christian must become a poet."

And that's what I've been attempting – mostly poorly – ever since, both in my life and in my music and my ministry: to be salt for the earth, light for the world, and "a finger pointing to the moon," as the Zen saying goes. It's a daily practice, and one I often fall short in, but I follow in the footsteps of others, and I take strength from their witness and all the guidance and love I know they still provide.

> "There is no such thing as an artist: there is only the world, lit or unlit as the light allows. When the candle is burning, who looks at the wick? When the candle is out, who needs it? But the world without light is wasteland and chaos, and a life without sacrifice is abomination." –Annie Dillard, "Holy the Firm"

As I write this – and most likely as you read it as well – the news is full of stories of mass shootings, war, pandemics, and escalating climate disasters worldwide. Sometimes I'm terrified to hit "refresh" on the news feed, but still can't stop myself from doom-scrolling through tale after tale of human brokenness, societal collapse, and the degradation of all of creation and the natural world.

I wish I could say that I meet all this tumultuousness with an outpouring of faith, hope, love and constant prayerfulness, but if I did I'd be lying. My father and mother certainly taught me *how* to pray – so there's no blaming them for my own shortcomings – and I've learned much more about prayer over the years as well from many spiritual teachers and guides, some living and some long-since departed this world. But my own life of prayer is a weak echo of theirs, pitiful really, and nothing to be emulated.

Instead, inspired by those dearest to me – like my mom, may her memory be eternal! – I meet the insanity and the terror of existence with song. Or I try to, at any rate. It's most likely a fool's errand, and not one I'd necessarily recommend — wielding melody, rhythm, and rhyme against the darkness that threatens to claim the hearts of us all. Music probably doesn't stand a chance, and yet, most days, it's all I've got. As the hymn says, "How can I keep from singing?"

Really – and let's be clear here – I have no business writing to tell you about prayer, or the Psalms. I struggle constantly with inconsistency in my own prayer life. My zeal comes and goes, my inspiration waxes and wanes, sometimes seasonally, sometimes by the hour. Some days I have all the words at the tip of my tongue, all the prayers I need planted deep in my heart and ready to bloom, while on many others I sit in frustrated silence and near-despondency, just hoping to muster up enough strength to affirm, one more time, God's presence in my life and in the world around me.

I've struggled with theodicy and the problem of evil at least since I was in high school. Spiritually speaking, I sometimes joke that I hit my midlife crisis sometime in my early 20s. I even toyed with unbelief for a time, thinking that might be easier than faith. But, for me at least, the arguments for materialism or nihilism always rang hollow, and I could never really convince myself to see the universe as purely mechanistic or disenchanted in any real sense. All it ever took was a walk in the woods, or an afternoon at the park, or a beautiful piece of music or poetry, to restore my faith. I was far too inconstant in my unbelief, too much in awe of the beauty all around me.

There is a deep unknowing, a sense of paradox and uncertainty, that comes as a constant corollary to the life of faith, but I've yet to find any satisfactory alternative, any surer ground to stand on. For now, then, this "cloud of unknowing" is my home, and like the Taoist sage Lieh Tzu I ride the wind, onward and upward, in search of new horizons and new songs to sing.

Few things in this life last, and it turned out that the Disciples of Christ church where I had found myself doing music for so many years – the church whose hundredth anniversary celebration I had attended along with my wife, her grandmother, and her family – was not meant to survive long into its second century. Changing times, a shrinking congregation, a global pandemic – all of these and more came together to bring an end to a church that had previously survived so much.

> O Lord, how manifold are thy works!
> In wisdom hast thou made them all. (Psalm 104:24)

This is one of the hardest parts to write about, because it's still so fresh. The wounds are still raw, still painful, and still healing. Our music crew at that little church was a small band – especially in those final days – but we gave it everything we had. We played and sang with all the heart we could muster, making a joyful noise until the very end, until that very last Sunday morning when we sang our last song together. I sometimes thought of us like the band playing on the deck of the Titanic, joining together for one last refrain of "Nearer My God to Thee" as the ship broke apart and sank.

> Yonder is the sea, great and wide,
> which teems with things innumerable,
> living things both small and great.
> There go the ships, and Leviathan which thou didst form
>   to sport in it. (Psalm 104:25-26)

Saint Augustine, in a commentary on Psalm 104, suggests that the ships are an image of the Christian churches, each traversing the sometimes-dangerous oceans in search of safe harbor and ultimate homecoming. Until the closing of the church in Houston, I had never before experienced a sense of loss quite like it. It was both my music ministry and a weekly way of expressing myself as a creative person in the world.

Through all the necessary compromises of my adult life – settling for a respectable day job, giving up so many of my youthful dreams of a life devoted to philosophy and literature and the arts, accepting the everyday beauty of the commonplace in exchange for the brightly flashing fires of artistic inspiration – my time in music ministry at that church was an anchor that kept me connected, even consecrated in some mysterious way, to something deep within myself, to some truth more true that that which most could see.

Without it, who was I, and what would I be? But, of course, as both the Book of Job and Psalm 104 remind us, the Lord gives and the Lord takes away, and through it all we bless God's holy name.

> These all look to thee,
> to give them their food in due season.
> When thou givest to them, they gather it up;
> when thou openest thy hand, they are filled with good things.
> When thou hidest thy face, they are dismayed;
> when thou takest away their breath, they die
> and return to their dust.
> When thou sendest forth thy Spirit, they are created;
> and thou renewest the face of the earth. (Psalm 104:27-30)

Only God knows what happens next. I think on some level this should be a relief, even if it doesn't always feel that way. The same God who sustains the created world is also sustaining and supporting us through all the trials and tribulations of our lives.

No matter how alone we may feel, Psalm 104 is a reminder to us that we live in an enchanted world – a world suffused with grace and the invisible energy of God's love for everything that ever was, is, or will be.

When my mom died, they asked if I would like to sing something at her funeral. At that point, I had been doing regular Sunday music ministry for many years, and I was experienced at singing and leading worship through all sorts of emotional states, through all life's various ups and downs. All the same, singing at her funeral was one of the most intense experiences I've ever had as a musician.

I decided on an *a capella* rendition of the haunting old Appalachian hymn "What Wondrous Love Is This." Thankfully, I managed to keep it together and made it through the song without breaking into tears, but the experience had a profound impact that stayed with me. I especially remember singing the song's last verse:

And when from death I'm free,
I'll sing on, I'll sing on,
And when from death I'm free, I'll sing on
And when from death I'm free, I'll sing and joyful be
And through eternity, I'll sing on, I'll sing on
And through eternity, I'll sing on

Coming just days after Easter, it was impossible not to contrast the solemnity of my mom's funeral mass with the joyful celebration of Christ's resurrection that had so shortly preceded it. And so, singing the verse that began, "And when from death I'm free," I found myself thinking not only of my mom, but also of Christ's harrowing of Hell and his utter destruction, once and for all, of the gates of Hades. As Saint Paul writes in 1 Corinthians 15, "O death, where is thy sting? O grave, where is thy victory?"

As hard as it is to accept, or even comprehend, in the hurried midst of our daily lives, there is a promise in this hymn and in these lines of scripture – that through the mystery of Christ's death and resurrection, we have absolutely nothing to fear. Not now, not ever.

My mom was an amazing person, an amazing musician and writer, and an amazing mother and friend. She gave so much of herself for others – for her family, her church, her community. I miss her so much, and there have definitely been times since her death when I haven't been sure I had the strength to go on without her wisdom and ongoing guidance, or to make good on her incredible legacy. But then I realize that she's still with me – always, and especially whenever I make music. Music connects me to her across time and space, across life and death, in a way that perhaps nothing else could.

Thinking back to all the memories of my mom and of our family making music together over the years, I realize she gave that gift of music to us – to me and my sisters and my dad – and now that gift, just like the free gift of God's grace, sustains and supports us and reminds us of her love and tender care, especially on the days when we most need it, when life is at its hardest and the way ahead seems most uncertain.

> Thou hast made the moon to mark the seasons;
> The sun knows its time for setting.
> Thou makest darkness, and it is night,
> When all the beasts of the forest creep forth.
> The young lions roar for their prey,
> Seeking their food from God.
> When the sun rises, they get them away and lie down in their dens.
> Man goes forth to his work and to his labor until the evening. (Psalm 104:19-23)

I tend to believe we're all doing the best we can in this life, each of us yearning for a truth and a transcendence that mostly eludes us in our day-to-day lives. Yet we go forth to our work and to our labor each day, trying to survive and make the best of it, but also trying to make the world a little bit better – and perhaps a little bit more beautiful – for our having passed this way. In the end, as Saint Paul says, we have love or we have nothing.

So I try to pray, to chant a few Psalms, to read the scriptures, and to sing as well as I can with the voice I've been given. I've even written a few songs and hymns of my own, something to leave along the path as I go, like breadcrumbs reminding myself of the way back home. When I can't sing, or when I can't find the words to pray, I enter into that great silence, and ask God to join me, once again, in the depths of my unknowing and uncertainty.

And when that final evening comes, when my work and my labors are finally done and my last song on Earth is finished, I look forward, in faith, to a Heavenly reunion, to joining once again with my mom in music – to make a joyful noise with her and with all those who have gone on ahead to light the way for us, to sing us all into glory with their unending hymns of thanksgiving, praise, and love.

Practice

Plant something beautiful in your mind

I'd like to make a case here for memorizing something beautiful, and then relishing the pleasure of reciting it and making a home for it in your mind and heart. It could be a Psalm, or a favorite prayer, or just a good poem. Whatever it is, it doesn't have to be long or overly complicated. If you love Shakespeare soliloquies, that's great, but if you find Elizabethan-era drama boring or inaccessible, try something by a contemporary poet instead, something written in a style you connect with but that's still rich with imagery and meaning.

There's an awful lot vying for space in our minds these days, but the things we commit to memory are the things we carry with us throughout our days and, ultimately, throughout our lives. In our age of superabundant, super-fast digital communication, I've found there's a temptation to be constantly filling my mind up with the news of the day, whether through traditional outlets or on social media. There seems to be so much of importance to keep up with that I often feel like I can't afford to close off that fire hose of information and input – no matter how exhausted I am, or how little time it leaves me to just be alone with my thoughts, or to enjoy a quiet moment of meditation or rest in the here and now.

One of the great challenges of our time, then, seems to be to find ways to slow down, to hit pause, take a breath, and step back. At the end of the day, it's up to us to preserve and tend the beauty of our own inner landscape. As Henry David Thoreau says in "Life Without Principle,"

> "We should treat our minds, that is, ourselves, as innocent and ingenuous children, whose guardians we are, and be careful what objects and what subjects we thrust on their attention. Read not the Times. Read the Eternities. ... Knowledge does not come to us by details, but in flashes of light from heaven."

In particular, the practice of memorizing passages from the Psalms has a rich tradition in the history of Christianity. It might be a project of a lifetime, but you have permission to start wherever you'd like and travel however far seems reasonable to you. Some people are sticklers about translations, but I'd say just find one that speaks to you and go for it. Whether it's the traditional language of the King James Version or Eugene Peterson's contemporary Message translation, you're bound to reap benefits from taking the time to learn and dwell in the language of these ancient poetic prayers that have made up the foundation of both Jewish and Christian worship for thousands of years.

Remember, though, that for the purposes of this practice, the goal isn't just to commit something to memory and then file it away, but to return to it at least with some kind of regularity, drawing on that treasure-store of memory to enter more and more deeply into the words of the Psalm or the poem, allowing them to wash over and through you and to impact the way you attend to the world, even to the most mundane aspects of your day-to-day life.

As it says in Romans 12:2, "Do not be conformed to this world, but be transformed by the renewing of your minds, so that you may discern what is the will of God—what is good and acceptable and perfect."

Experimenting with this practice, you might be surprised how even the most ordinary moments of life can be transformed – re-enchanted, even – by setting them against the backdrop of something beautiful, rich, and eternally true.

Chapter 10

Moving from Head to Heart in our call to Care for Creation

*W*e approach life differently because unique experiences have shaped us. Yet we all share this one home that God created. We share the common bond as creatures of the Creator. So to honor our differences and to explore our collective responsibility for our one home, we chose to each write a short piece about how our care for the earth shifted from knowledge to relationship. As you read our stories, we invite you to add yours.

Rev. Dr. Amber Mattingly:

Psalm 19: 1-6

The heavens tell of the glory of God;
And their expanse declares the work of His hands.
Day to day pours forth speech,
And night to night reveals knowledge.
There is no speech, nor are there words;
Their voice is not heard.
Their line has gone out into all the earth,
And their words to the end of the world.
In them He has placed a tent for the sun,
Which is like a groom coming out of his chamber;
Like a strong man that runs his course with joy!
Its rising is from]one end of the heavens,

And its circuit to the other end of them;
And there is nothing hidden from its heat.

I did not grow up in a church or a home that talked much about caring for the earth. I don't remember being led in worship or in a youth group to consider earth care as a part of stewardship. The earth was definitely something to delight in but I was not introduced to the idea that the earth and all of its beautiful creatures know God so well that they pour forth speech about God. I did not receive this message until after becoming a mother.

It seems that my children came out of the womb with a cry for creation care. My son was introduced to recycling at a young age and became an advocate for our home being a place that was more thoughtful about our purchasing of items in plastic and what could or could not be put into the recycling bin. My daughter talked to the squirrels and the leaves, communicating with them in a very natural way. One day, we were walking on a trail near our house and a large leaf fell from the tree onto her head. She took the large leaf off her head and with a giggle and a sparkle in her eye said to the leaf, "My dear friend, you hit me in the head! Let us walk a gentler path of nonviolence." Then, off she skipped down the path. I thought to myself, "Whose children am I raising? Might they be teachers sent for me?"

As our family continued to learn and add practices that focused on creation care, we were doing a lot of good things with this knowledge, but it felt strangely disconnected from a relationship with nature. What I mean is it started to feel like a checklist that I could mark off, but it had not impacted my heart in a deeply meaningful way. I was looking for a movement of my heart that might produce a love that would be the energy that moved me to care for creation like I would a family member.

Psalm 104 ends with the writer declaring that he has experienced the God who created and continuously reveals through the things God created. God knows us like a family member. This psalmist seems to get it! The writer connects all of creation to the intimate relationship of family.

During my research for my doctoral project, I studied a story that helped me shift from my creation care checklist to a heartfelt relationship. My research involved looking at the Hagar narrative in Genesis 16-21. This story is about one of the most vulnerable in the community. Hagar is a female in a male world, a stranger to the ways of Abraham's family, a foreigner from the land of Egypt, and a slave who doesn't even have rights to her body. The story goes that Abraham and Sarah are old and childless but God tells them that they will have children. So, Abraham and Sarah decide that God must have meant for them to use Hagar to give them a child. This is a terrifying story because Hagar is a woman whose body, the smallest land that she occupies, is violated for the sake of bearing the child promised to Abraham and Sarai. Riet Bons-Storm discusses how people's identities are connected to the body which is the smallest land they inhabit, and their unique holistic expression of themselves that empowers choices, and the place on earth where they live.[32] At the end of the story, Hagar is cast out of the community, but God who created Hagar and the land, hears her cry & responds by caring for Hagar like she is family. God provides water & refuge in the desert.

For years, my heart has repeated the phrase "the smallest land that I occupy." You see, my friends, if I am disconnected from, do not care for, and cannot love "the smallest land that I occupy" i.e. my body, then my love for the land on which I live will simply be a set of rules that I follow. The sustaining energy of love comes from first loving "the smallest land that I occupy" by listening to its need for good foods, by conversing with myself with compassion and not as a brutal taskmaster, and celebrating times of rest instead of demanding I keep producing. The practice of listening to "the smallest land that I occupy" is what will help me hear the

---

32   Riet Bons-Storm, "A place to share: Some Thoughts about the Meaning of Territory and Boundaries in our Thinking about God and Humanity," *HTS: Theological Studies* 64, no. 1 (2008): 144-145.

heavens declaring the glory of God and the skies proclaiming the work of God's hands."

Rev. Amanda Hines:

Ecology is defined as "the branch of science concerned with the interrelationship of organisms and their environments." I was not exposed to the complexity of ecology until I took a class titled "creation care as spiritual practice" while I was in seminary. One of the first exercises I did with my classmates was to exegete the word "care." To my surprise, I discovered that the etymology of the word "care" has connections to expressions of lament and grief. I had never thought about how caring for something means that we also open ourselves up to the possibility of grief and lament.

I began to wonder how every time God extends care to the earth and its creatures how often God has also experienced grief and lament for it all too. Based on this, I think that our connection, or perhaps reconnection, to the earth and all of creation teaches us more about being human and what it means to relate to the one that we call Lord, Creator, and Sustainer.

Throughout the bible, we discover places where creation praises God. We are able to read the ways that the heavens declare God's glory and how creation proclaims God's goodness. Hymns are also places where we can discover rich theology through lyrics and music and tunes that we hold close in our hearts.

As I reflected on the topic of creation care, my heart was drawn to the hymn "All Creatures of Our God and King" of which the lyrics were written by Saint Francis of Assisi. The founder of the Franciscans takes the individual through a rich language of the ways in which creation worships God. One thing that stands out is the way he writes how all created things praise God. Humans are given the unique gift of speech to be able to sing praises, but they are not the only ones who worship. The sun, moon, clouds, waters, and other elements are all given space and attention to worship their Creator. St. Francis reveals this larger picture of worship that places the human person in cooperation and partnership with the rest of creation. He reveals the ecology between humans and all other created things with the sole purpose to proclaim God's majesty.

The fifth verse sticks out as St. Francis also raises the notion of forgiveness. In its context, it seems that forgiveness is to be extended from one person to another, but I wonder if St. Francis was hinting at something larger.

The literature on the intersection between ecology and theology continues to grow, and I would like to suggest that St. Francis points Christian people to the practice of forgiveness through the lyrics of this hymn. I think in order for the modern Christian to engage responsibly and appropriately to the realities of ecological crisis the first step is to ask for forgiveness from God and from creation. Creation's pinnacle was not the creation of humans, but the consecration of Sabbath as a day for all things to rest and worship. There is no denying that humans have been the major cause for the current ecological concerns, and St. Francis articulates that forgiveness must be extended and the pain and sorrow that all of creation bears can be cast onto God.

It is fascinating to consider how animated and intimate our interconnectedness with creation is. Creation is personified in scripture and hymns to reveal the shared practices of worship, care, and forgiveness. If we are to fully embrace what it means to be created, we must begin acknowledging the One who sustains it all. We must be willing to open ourselves up to the possibility of heartache. And, we must authentically embrace the continual practice of forgiveness as it works to heal the deepest wounds that humanity and creation enact and witness.

Ngakpa Dawa Norbu:

When I was still serving as a pastor and still living in Wisconsin, I was talking one day with my spiritual director about renewal and refreshment. We were talking specifically about recovering from Sunday mornings.

He asked me, "What do you do when you get home on Sunday?"

"Watch football," I answered.

He said, "Does that really help you to feel refreshed?"

"Well, if the Packers are winning!" I responded.

I realized then that watching football was perhaps not the best way to re-gather my energy. There were more beneficial ways of relaxing, ways that reached deeper places in me, even that arose from within me. But sometimes those practices take more energy than I seem to have or more time than I want to give at the moment.

I think many of us have those "quicker-picker-uppers." It might be watching football or binging on a show or eating our favorite ice cream. In a sense, in those moments, we are taking refuge in the NFL or in Netflix or in Breyers. We are stepping out of whatever demands we have been facing and gaining some mental distance from them, but we are doing so more as an escape rather than as a retreat.

True retreat requires a more reliable refuge as well as a deeper aspiration. Winning football teams come and go. Television programs come to an end. The satisfaction we get from our favorite food slowly disappears. And the desire to feel better right now simply will not sustain us for very long. We need a refuge that is trustworthy, and we need an inner hope that will carry us far beyond the needs of the moment.

The call to, "Be still and know," offers this kind of refuge. It is a refuge that goes far beyond distraction or busyness or passing pleasure. It is a refuge that anchors us deep in our hearts, where our most important values and aspirations are. It is a place where profound calm may be found and where we remember why we are here – not just for ourselves, but for others; and not just for a few, but for all.

Many feel that the environmental threats to our planet scream for immediate action. And there is no underestimating the urgency of the peril we face. Lest we afflict the world, however, with our own anger, anxiety and confusion, it is vital that people who walk a spiritual path take time to seek inner guidance. Then, rather than responding with the energy of negative emotions, we can speak and act with a calm that spreads equanimity. We can speak and act with confidence that nothing can separate us from what we hold most dear and what holds us most dear. We can speak and act from a place of deep caring, for the earth and for all who inhabit it.

Be still and know. In this way the planet is healed, and in this way, we are healed with it.

Andre Brown

Our faith practice is personal.

I never knew that. I thought our faith was to be shared and that everyone had to agree. Like a contract. This is what we agree prayer is. This is what we all believe salvation is. This is what sin is and so on. I mean it makes sense. We all use the same title, "Christian" so we should in theory believe the same exact thing. I heard the word error used often in church. And I don't want to be wrong or in error, so it's best to do what the preacher says. Whatever your pastor says is wrong or in error then those things ought to be avoided. Our faith feels simple in that way. Do what is right and don't do what is wrong. It seems simple enough.

But what is right and what is wrong? As Hamlet says, 'ay, there's the rub'. What does God require from us? What does God want from me? To be nice? To be good? To be polite? To be quiet? To stay out the way? To not make waves? These were questions I had for such a long time. I didn't know who to ask. I couldn't ask God because I was told never to question him. But it never resolved those quandaries.

One of the first major questions I had was, "everyone has to believe in jesus?" That was so disturbing. "What about Muslims?" I thought. "What about all my Jewish friends?" Everyone who doesn't believe in Jesus is going to Hell? For years I silently struggled with that idea. My only saving grace is that I had more Christian friends so it became an easier pill to swallow, but I also think I did this weird thing in my heart where I just stopped believing that was true. I did my own theology. and guess what, we all do. Think about it, has anyone ever fully explained why bad things happen to good people sufficiently? Or why doesn't God systematically wipe out all of the evil folks with the blink of his eye, so we can all live in peace and harmony? Right. It's because our faith is personal. It works for us. We employ our faith in the ways that we need to live, to thrive and to love.

Our faith practice is personal. It's customized to work in tandem with our mind and heart. It expands in ways we can't imagine; it can grow; it can be created; it can join with others but it always remains ours. Our faith can hold the unimaginable which is why there can be ten people in the same service and they can all have vastly different experiences.

What this means is you build the faith practice for the life you want to have. You get to have the life of faith you desire. It will fit. It will work. It is customizable.

Coming home to yourself means that as a person of faith you get to decide what kind of life of faith you will lead. Perhaps you will pray in the morning. Perhaps you won't. Maybe you'll kneel at night or maybe not. Maybe you'll pray before you eat a meal, maybe not. Maybe you will sing worship songs all day. Maybe you will read self help books and feel rejuvenated and make small changes in your life for the better. Maybe you will give money to the poor. Maybe you will feed the hungry or volunteer with children on the weekends. Maybe you will offer counsel to friends and pray with them in secret. Maybe you will support missions in other countries. Maybe you will sing in your church choir. Perhaps you will meditate often on the state of the world and wish for better. Perhaps you love to bake and you bring sweets to communities you are a part of. Or maybe you're a writer and you send cards, notes and well wishes to friends when they least expect. Maybe you only write in your journal.

To live in this world and to be human and to experience your humanity alongside others is to witness a spiritual journey that in many cases requires faith. It requires elements of life that we cannot see. But above all else, there must be love. 1 Cor 13:12, "For now we see only a reflection as in a mirror; then we shall see face to face. Now I know in part; then I shall know fully, even as I am fully known. And now these three remain: faith, hope and love, but the greatest of these is love."

Recently, a friend asked me what practices I do to take care of my spirit and reconnect with the earth. Her father is a minister and she decided she would no longer attend his church because her beliefs had shifted. I gave her a litany of things I do to remain connected to spirit. I told her that I pray in different ways. I use songs as meditation and focused thoughts as prayer. I journal my gratitude and say thank you to the universe out loud often. But I felt like my response wasn't nearly good enough. In what ways am I being a steward of the resources God has given me in the earth? Romans 8:19 declares, "...For creation eagerly awaits the revealing of the [children] of God." Earth has an expectation for our authenticity. Our worship to God is in our hands and our feet. Although our hearts may be filled with compassion, we are called to eagerly engage in earth-work. Earth's work is justice. It's proclaiming the good news to the poor, fighting for freedom for prisoners, teaching those who are lost in ignorance, setting the oppressed free and declaring that freedom for all people. Psalm 24:1 says "The earth is the Lord's and the fullness thereof, the world and those who dwell therein..." When we partner in the work of earth, we partner with the divine.

Angela Patterson

I'll be honest – I didn't really think too much about the environment until James Cone told me I should.

Almost 25 years ago, the famed theologian wrote a piece called "Whose Earth Is It Anyway", which argues that those who are passionate about achieving racial equity and those who fight to save the earth may want to walk a mile in each others' shoes. Cone points out that the horrors of racism and environmental injustice are inextricably linked, as communities of color are disproportionately home to landfills, toxic waste dumps and the like. To have healthy ecosystems only in the suburbs will never save the planet from environmental ruin. Conversely, Cone calls those involved in climate justice and the like to examine the culture responsible for this ecological crisis – and see that the white supremacy embedded there might be to blame for both the evils of racism and harm to the earth.[33]

Sadly, as a biracial black person, it had never occurred to me that to care for our environment is to support people of color, and to work toward racial equity is to also right environmental wrongs. Because you can't fix one without the other.

As I continued on my spiritual journey, I began to understand more about the ties to and importance of nature in religious and spiritualities native to people of color. It wasn't just that the environment is sometimes used as a way to physically eradicate a people, but is perhaps used more swiftly (and shrewdly) to smother their religious and spiritual lives, which is a cruel death in and of itself. To preserve our environments is core to keeping our connections to God intact.

It was learning about Native American spirituality and traditions that taught me the earth is not ours to steward, but more accurately to be in communion with. When we give back to the earth it not only gives back to us, but it also offers us a place and space to connect with each other. Damaging the planet is just another way to separate us from one another. Robin Wall Kimmerer, author of Braiding Sweetgrass, said:

---

33   J. H. Cone, "Whose earth is it anyway?" *Cross Currents*, 50(1/2), 36-
      46.

"The Honorable Harvest asks us to give back, in reciprocity, for what we have been given. Reciprocity helps resolve the moral tension of taking a life by giving in return something of value that sustains the ones who sustain us. One of our responsibilities as human people is to find ways to enter into reciprocity with the more-than-human world. We can do it through gratitude, through ceremony, through land stewardship, science, art, and in everyday acts of practical reverence."[34]

For me, creation care is just that – repairing, supporting and uplifting all of creation so each living being can thrive. This goes way beyond advocating for legislation, protesting wrongs, demanding action from our representatives – all of which is necessary. It also means that we are called to recognize the fact that each of us is inextricably linked. Our fates are tied together, despite how separate we may feel from the soul next to us. If we're able to get out of our own way to do that, Cone's call to look through the other's lens may be easier to do, and then we might win the struggle to save all of us.

Courtney Armento

When we have trouble praying, Teresa recommends that we turn to nature: "Go to some place where you can see the sky, and walk up and down a little." Since God is infinite and everywhere, sometimes we rejoice as much in meditating on creation as in meditating on the Divine. —Tessa Bielecki[35]

This reflection, based on St. Teresa of Avila's life, is a perfect springboard into consideration for the earth. If we think of earth and all of life as sacred, a reflection or expression of the Holy, then it becomes easy to find the Holy ground upon which we stand a gift. We can connect to nature in a new way. Maybe as we inhale

---

34   Kimmerer, R.W. *Braiding sweetgrass.* (Minneapolis, MN: Milkweed Editions. 2013), 190..

35   https://cac.org/daily-meditations/zest-for-life-love-for-creation-2023-03-16/

we consider, this earth is alive, it is a breathing, living, part of all of us and God is enmeshed with it and with us.

I recently found myself weeding at the church I serve. I was angry at how the plants we were weeding around had come into being. Someone decided these plants were what we needed and planted them without conversation or consensus of the collective. So I was not joyfully and gratefully going about this task. I might have even grumbled at the whole situation. I accidentally pulled some living plant parts when pulling weeds. When I realized that, I began to put these living vibrant plant bodies in a small pile so that we could replant them. Now, I care about them in a new way. I connected with their life source energy that is breath and I saw their beauty and value. When the task had been completed for the day, I went back for the plant bodies that had been laid so carefully on the side for follow up care. They were nowhere to be found. Someone scooped them up and placed them in the trash. My heart was sad. I had finally come home to myself by recognizing the life in the plant was connected to all of life and enmeshed with the Holy. I began to feel gratitude for the plants and realized how precious all life is. I wondered how the plant parts would feel as they lost their home, their grip and connection to life, the sun, the rain, the clouds for relief from the sun. My capacity for appreciation for all living things grew. I knew I cared about people and animals and the earth before, but because of this experience, something new shifted in me. God meets us in nature. God offers us beauty unparalleled for space to find God, to commune with life, to find joy, to find balance with life and to even find rest.

When you are able, go outside and plant your feet firmly on the ground. Take in the scenery, find a focal point of beauty and Breathe in gratitude, Breathe out abundance. Breathe in the Holy, Breathe out loving care. Breathe in joy, Breathe out ease. Breathe in expansion, Breathe out heaviness. Amen

Michael Esterheld

> "If I do not feel a sense of joy in God's creation, if I forget to offer the world back to God with thankfulness, I have advanced very little upon the Way. I have not yet learnt to be truly human. For it is only through thanksgiving that I can become myself."
> — Kallistos Ware, "The Orthodox Way"

> "To be enlightened is to become intimate with all things."
> — Zen saying

The mythologist, scholar, and storyteller Martin Shaw, in his book "Smokehole: Looking to the Wild in the Time of the Spyglass," recounts the old folk tale of The Handless Maiden. It's a gruesome and frightening tale in spots, but then these times of ours can also be gruesome and frightening, and we needn't necessarily turn our faces away from old stories like these that might be rich with meaning and metaphors to inform our own individual and collective journeys.

I wouldn't want to spoil it for you, but I will say that the tale of the Handless Maiden has its share of loss, sadness, disempowerment, and grief, but also glorious measures of compassion, unyielding love, and the fervent hope of ultimate restoration. Near the end of his commentary on the tale, Shaw sends up a kind of prayer on behalf of present-day readers and our troubled world.

"I send a voice," Shaw writes, "that as cultures, humans, parents, brothers and sisters, whiskery ones, settled ones, unsettled ones, ones that are more crow than girl, more antelope than boy – the whole lot of us – grow our own hands back, so this beauteous earth can start to do the same."

One element that is absolutely crucial to restoration in the tale is the life-giving and life-restoring magic of community – of shared lives, shared sorrows and passions and joys, of music and meals and lively dancing enjoyed together in common, and in the close proximity of the natural world.

Another crucial element is the natural world itself, including the dark and foreboding forest – initially a place of exile and wandering – which eventually becomes the very place of restoration and reunion, the place where we go to experience healing and come into a more intimate communion with who we truly are while reclaiming the fundamental truths that bind us all together.

"We make things holy," Shaw says, "by the kind of attention we give them." It might benefit each of us, then, to put down our smartphones, walk away from our screens, step outside, and see once more the real, unmitigated world around us — to step boldly into whatever passes for our own personal wilderness, and to learn once more how to attend to what we find there, including the deep stirrings of our own hearts.

I don't know whether we can actually turn the corner and recommit ourselves to caring for this Earth in time to save civilization as we now know it. But, as Shaw concludes the passage quoted above, "If you're going to make a prayer, might as well make it a big one."

www.ingramcontent.com/pod-product-compliance
Lightning Source LLC
Chambersburg PA
CBHW021234090426
42740CB00006B/522

Advance Praise for *Finding Rest for Our Souls*

Mattingly and her colleagues vulnerably offer their own journeys of healing as they invite readers to rituals and practices that facilitate deep, soul-renewing rest. The integration of theology, experiences, and application is a rare find. This book is for anyone willing to be more whole.

Rev. Dr. Dawn Weaks
author of *Breakthrough: Trusting God for Big Change in Your Church*

"The collective Church is looking for where God is moving, aching for something that has been missing inside the walls of the institution, and desperate for answers for the division in the world. *Finding Rest for Our Souls* is a brave and deeply moving collection of leaders sharing their vulnerable stories of searching and finding the mystery of God again. From challenging the incomplete man-made disciplines to the awareness of our participation with creation, the authors' challenge us all to expand our hearts, slow down, and learn to be truly present with ourselves and God again. If you feel something is missing in your relationship with yourself or God, if your spiritual disciplines have become stale, or if you have been wondering if there is something more, *Finding Rest for Our Souls* is a moving place to begin."

Corie Weathers, LPC, NCC, BCC
Military Clinical Consultant | Author | Lifegiver, LLC